The Reverse Mortgage Advantage

The Tax-Free, House-Rich Way to Retire Wealthy!

WARREN BOROSON

McGraw-Hill

New York Chicago San Francisco Lisbon London
Madrid Mexico City Milan New Delhi San Juan
Seoul Singapore Sydney Toronto

1 2 3 4 5 6 7 8 9 0   DOC/DOC   0 9 8 7 6

ISBN 0-07-147072-7

This publication is designed to provide accurate and authoritative information in regard to the subject matter covered. It is sold with the understanding that neither the author nor the publisher is engaged in rendering legal, accounting, or other professional service. If legal advice or other expert assistance is required, the services of a competent professional person should be sought.

> —*From a declaration of principles jointly adopted by a committee*
> *of the American Bar Association and a committee of publishers*

McGraw-Hill books are available at special quantity discounts to use as premiums and sales promotions, or for use in corporate training programs. For more information, please write to the Director of Special Sales, McGraw-Hill Professional, Two Penn Plaza, New York, NY 10121-2298. Or contact your local bookstore.

 This book is printed on recycled, acid-free paper containing a minimum of 50% recycled, de-inked fiber.

Library of Congress Cataloging-in-Publication Data

Boroson, Warren.
  The reverse mortgage advantage : the tax-free, house-rich way to retire wealthy! / by Warren Boroson.
    p. cm. MAR 07 *332.722*
    Includes index.
    ISBN 0-07-147072-7 (alk. paper) *B645r*
  1. Mortgage loans, Reverse. 2. Home equity conversion. 3. Retirement income.
I. Title.
  HG2040.15.B6698 2006
  332.7'22—dc22

                         2006013615

To Rebecca, Bram, and Matthew

Contents

Contents

Preface

Reverse mortgages are a fairly new wrinkle, and dramatic changes are sure to come in the years ahead. For instance, other lenders will probably arrive on the scene to offer such mortgages to people whose houses are above-average in value, not just average in value or extremely high in value. After all, it is not just ordinary people who may be house-rich and cash-poor; very wealthy people may be exceedingly house-rich and somewhat cash-poor. As someone has said, reverse mortgages are a work in progress. One recent important change: The Department of Housing and Urban Development now allows counselors from the National Foundation of Credit Counselors and Money Management International to provide guidance about its Home Equity Conversion Mortgage.

But reverse mortgages are certainly an idea whose time has come, despite all the myths and misinformation that have been circulating out there—myths and misinformation that, I hope, this book will help in some small measure to dispel.

The Reverse Mortgage Advantage

The Tax-Free,
House-Rich Way to
Retire Wealthy!

Introduction

A Most Peculiar Mortgage

If you are somewhat nervous about the whole idea of a reverse mortgage—where you borrow against your free-and-clear ownership of your home—welcome to the club!

Almost anybody would be nervous.

Besides which, a good many scary and misleading stories have been circulating about reverse mortgages (see Chapter 3). Perhaps the most common and the most nasty: A bank will take over your house, and you will wind up out on the street or perhaps living with your disgruntled children.

Not that reverse mortgages are always the best step for any older homeowner in pursuit of cash. There are reasonable alternatives, such as a home-equity loan, moving to a smaller residence in a less expensive community, or buying an income (immediate) annuity (see Chapter 5). Still, much of the time, when you add up the pros and the cons, the reverse mortgage manages to land in the winner's circle.

It is, after all, a most peculiar mortgage.

It isn't simply the opposite of a "forward" mortgage, not just a mortgage where a bank pays you instead of your paying the bank.

It is a mortgage where you can't ever be left holding the bag. Even if you get a reverse mortgage at 62 and live to 104, and the monthly payments you receive total $1 million while your house is worth only $300,000, you won't owe the bank any more than $300,000. Neither will your children or any other heirs you may have.

A very peculiar mortgage, as I said.

Yes, reverse mortgages have drawbacks. They are not a primrose path to Easy Street.

Here are some of those drawbacks:

- If you have a very expensive house, you may have trouble getting a lot of money from a government-sponsored reverse mortgage. Such reverse mortgages are for the average American, not for the Bill Gateses of the world. (But there are other reverse mortgages for the Gateses, called cash accounts. A woman with an $18 million house got one. See Chapter 11.)
- Reverse mortgages are not cheap. They come with expensive "closing costs," the money you must fork over to get the mortgage. I know a former banker, in her 80s, who took one look at the closing costs of a reverse mortgage she was applying for and snorted, "Outrageous!" She was wrong. But even leaders in the reverse-mortgage world concede that nobody ever said they were cheap.

Why aren't reverse mortgages more popular? More and more people have been getting them, but many more people would benefit. Here are some of the reasons:

- They are relatively new, dating back only a few decades.
- They are sometimes hard to understand. There are a few varieties, for one thing, and they play by somewhat different rules.
- They can be intimidating, introducing people to strange words like HECM, LIBOR indexes, and tenure periods.
- There have always been scandals involving mortgages. At one time, for example, there were "shared appreciation" mortgages. You obtained a loan on your house, and when the house eventually was sold, the lender helped himself to a percentage of the house's appreciation. Some lenders hired appraisers who deliberately under-appraised the value of a house—so that the lenders grabbed a

higher percentage of the sales price than they were entitled to. Today, shared-appreciation mortgages are typically not administered. And most reverse mortgages are carefully monitored by the U.S. Department of Housing and Urban Development to prevent any hanky-panky.

Now let us look at some good things about reverse mortgages:

- A poll of people 55 and older by the AARP found that 89 percent wanted to stay where they were living as long as possible. One of the primary benefits of a reverse mortgage is that you can remain in your house. The chances of your leaving your house against your will are very slim. To lose your house, involuntarily, you would have to stop paying the property taxes or neglect your house something awful. And when that has seemed a possibility, lenders usually step in to prevent this.
- The second major benefit of a reverse mortgage is that you can readily access cash when you need it.
- There's a good chance that your heirs will still inherit some money, even if you borrow against your house to the hilt. It's rare for houses in America to lose their value over any long time period. So, if you live in your house for any decent length of time after getting a reverse mortgage, its value is likely to appreciate—beyond the amount that you borrowed plus any interest you owe.
- Today's reverse mortgages are much simpler and more attractive than they were in the past. Today, certain expenses have limits on them. People applying for reverse mortgages must be given advice from counselors who are knowledgeable and objective. In short, it's a brand-new and far better ballgame, demonstrating why the number of reverse mortgages doubled from 2003 to 2004.
- In the early 1980s, I was writing about reverse mortgages and recall Jack Guttentag of the Wharton School, a mortgage expert, telling me what a good idea reverse mortgages were, if only they would cost less. Today they do cost less, and I will demonstrate the ways to further reduce costs (see Chapter 14).
- Finally, a reverse mortgage can make life much nicer and more comfortable for older Americans. Extra cash can mean that older

folks can more readily pay their bigger bills—their property taxes, home maintenance, and insurance. They can afford better health care and more comprehensive health insurance. They can buy newer and safer cars, dine out more often at better restaurants, take longer vacations and travel overseas, offer money for college to their grandchildren, and go to bed at night without fretting about unpaid bills.

Basically, a reverse mortgage can help older people live more comfortably and relax. The reaction I have heard again and again from people who have obtained reverse mortgages is that it was a godsend.

Thomas Scabareti, an authority on reverse mortgages, has summed it up nicely: "They are not a panacea. They are right for some people and not right for others. If you need additional income for a period of time, it's a good product. The terms are favorable, and there are great protections to let you age in place. For a lot of people, they work."

Even if you are persuaded that a reverse mortgage is just the ticket for you, or for a parent or relative, questions remain. What kind of payment do you want—a lump sum, monthly checks, a line of credit, or a combination? Which lender should you get a reverse mortgage from? And how can you keep the fees and other charges down?

In this book I have tried to provide sensible and easy-to-understand answers to these questions. As an old-timer myself, my goal is to share wisdom and tactics so that you can obtain the right reverse mortgage for your situation.

I've featured interviews with many esteemed authorities on reverse mortgages, including lenders, government officials, and people who have actually taken out reverse mortgages. (Some of the interviews with borrowers were conducted by Mia Paterno, Iris Rosendahl, Mary Linley, Bram Boroson, and Rebecca Boroson; editing was done by Matthew Boroson.)

In addition to providing practical information about reverse mortgages, I suggest how to spend the money you receive—and most importantly, how *not* to spend the money to avoid financial troubles (chapters 15 and 16). Advice is also offered to the adult children of borrowers, beginning with: Don't feel guilty if you want an inheritance (Chapter 18).

Finally, my credentials: As a former real estate agent, I have received numerous awards from prominent real estate organizations. I understand mortgages, having been a homeowner for more than 40 years. My writing includes articles on everything from the care and feeding of septic tanks (*Money* magazine) to how to bargain for a house (*New York Daily News* magazine). Books I've written on real estate include *How to Buy a House with Nothing (or Little) Down* (with Martin M. Shenkman), *How to Sell Your House in a Buyer's Market* (with Mr. Shenkman), *The Homebuyer's Inspection Guide* (with Ken Austin), *Save Thousands on Your Mortgage, Sell Your Own Home, Everything You Need to Know About Buying a House (in 60 Pages),* and *Buying and Selling a House in a Changing Market.*

As you proceed through the reverse mortgage selection process, I would be pleased to hear from you, learn about your own experiences, and answer any questions you may have. Feel free to e-mail me at: WarrenBoroson@aol.com.

1

Reverse Mortgages for Total Beginners

Here are several questions that people have asked about reverse mortgages, along with the answers.

Can you explain what a reverse mortgage is so that I can finally understand it?

I knew a violinist with the New York Philharmonic who had most of his financial assets in two rare violins: a Stradivarius and a Guarnieri. They were worth, together, over $1 million. But his portfolio, while noteworthy, was not diversified. If the market for rare violins sank, his worldly wealth would have been devastated.

His portfolio was also illiquid; if he needed cash, it's doubtful that he could quickly sell one of his violins for a reasonable price.

A house is like that. Valuable and illiquid. If you are willing to take a big loss, you could probably find a buyer in no time, but, even so, getting your hands on the money would still take months.

Assuming that the violinist needed cash, he might have obtained a loan, with his violins as collateral. He would receive money—and he would still own those violins, which he needs for his job.

That's what homeowners with reverse mortgages have done—obtained a loan secured by their houses. But they must eventually repay the loan, with interest.

Will I still own my house?

Absolutely!

"That's the No. 1 question people ask me," says Sarah Hulbert, senior vice president, national director, of Seattle Mortgage Company's Reverse Mortgage Division, "and for 14 years I've been giving the same answer. Of course you will."

This is the most pernicious myth about reverse mortgages—that a bank or the government will end up owning your home sweet home.

When Bill Agner, director of reverse mortgages for the Mortgage Network in Indianapolis, gives a talk, an unhappy listener will invariably say to him afterwards, "Yeah, you get a few bucks, and then they take your home."

Fortunately, people seem to be becoming better informed. These days, when Mike Gruley, president of First Financial Mortgage Corp. in Northville, Michigan, asks audiences how many people believe that banks will wind up owning the homes of borrowers with reverse mortgages, only 5 percent raise their hands. Not long ago, it was 80 percent.

Well, yes, it's possible that you can lose your house. In very unusual situations—if you don't pay the property taxes or keep up your home-owners insurance, or if you let your home deteriorate badly (we're not just talking about ordinary wear and tear).

But Gruley notes that lenders will be very cautious when it comes to evicting people from their houses; a lender needs the Department of Housing and Urban Development's permission to do so. "And HUD is unlikely to kick an old widow out of her house," he says. The publicity would give the entire reverse-mortgage industry, still in its infancy, a hurt that would not heal quickly.

In fact, no one I have interviewed knows of anyone who has obtained a reverse mortgage and wound up being evicted. If a borrower does fall behind on property taxes or insurance, lenders may pay the bills them-selves—by lowering the amount being loaned to the homeowner.

Who can get a reverse mortgage?

Someone 62 or older with a house that is his or her main residence and who has received counseling and has a certificate to prove it.

Who should get one?

One ideal candidate is someone who is "house-rich and cash-poor." Like the man with the two violins. And anyone with a continual need for money, not just a colossal need right now. "Continual" is the key word. Other ideal candidates are people who *want* cash—to live a more comfortable life. They are not the same as people who *need* cash.

Where do you get a reverse mortgage?

The big three: the Department of Housing and Urban Development is behind the Home Equity Conversion Mortgage (HECM); Fannie Mae has its Home Keeper; and Financial Freedom has its Cash Account.

For a free list of reverse mortgage lenders and certified loan-counseling agencies, contact HUD at 888-466-3487. For information about lenders that offer Fannie Mae Home Keeper reverse mortgages, call 800-732-6643. For information about Financial Freedom Cash Accounts, call 888-REVERSE. Also, the National Reverse Mortgage Association Act at 1-866-264-4466.

How much can I get?

That depends on your age, the value of the house, and the level of interest rates. The older you are, the more valuable the house, and the lower interest rates are, the more you can borrow. In 2006, the maximum lending limits were:

HECM = $200,160 (mostly rural areas) to $362,790 (urban)

Fannie Mae Home Keeper = $417,200

Financial Freedom Cash Account = No set limit

Who should not get one?

First off, someone thinking of living in a house for only a few years—such as a person planning to move to a warmer climate soon. Reason: those closing costs may not have been worth it.

This example has been calculated by the National Center for Home Equity Conversion: A 75-year-old widow gets a $150,000 reverse mortgage, folding the $6,500 closing costs into the loan. She then begins receiving a monthly income of $562. Two years later, she moves to a nursing home. Over two years, the monthly income she received was $13,488. Considering the closing costs and the interest she owed, her effective interest rate was almost 50 percent. But if she had lived in the house for 12 years, receiving $80,928, the effective interest rate would have dropped to 10.8 percent.

Why the age of 62?

Perhaps because most Americans retire at age 62. Also, as Sarah Hulbert points out, people under 62 have such long life expectancies that the size of the loan available to them might not be significant.

Why have reverse mortgages not become more popular?

In many cases, widows are the ideal borrowers, but they tend not to be knowledgeable about finance and therefore are full of trepidation because their late husbands handled all the finances. With a widow, says Agner, "We try to bring in other family members to help her."

Another reason is that older people tend to be dubious about debt. They remember the Depression, when banks foreclosed on houses right and left. And not long ago these same homeowners celebrated when their mortgages were finally paid up. (In the old days, there were actually mortgage-burning parties.) No wonder that people in their 60s or older become anxious at the thought of obtaining a new mortgage.

Baby boomers, people born right after World War II, are more open to the idea. They are the credit card generation, and debt has never daunted them.

Not only that, but Joseph DeMarkey, vice president of the Bank of New York Mortgage in Milford, Massachusetts, believes they are not so intent on leaving a large estate. Whereas many older people want to leave their houses to their children.

John Curtis, Wells Fargo home mortgage area manager in the Minneapolis area, reports that the children may be living in $500,000 houses and making $500,000 a year, but their parents want these kids to inherit the family homestead. He asks these parents: "Did your own mom and dad leave you anything?" "Nope." He winds up advising them to take care of themselves. (*Minneapolis Star Tribune*, Sept. 7, 2002)

Still another reason that reverse mortgages are not more popular is that the subject is complicated. You have a variety of choices, and there are darned few easy answers. One counselor, Stephen Pepe of the Community Service Network in Stoneham, Massachusetts, tells me that many of his clients ask him, "If your parents applied for a loan, what would you tell them?" His sensible answer: it depends on their situation.

Do people use the money frivolously?

In places where house prices have soared, an increasing number of people do use their extra money for luxuries, like trips down the Amazon or to buy expensive Ferraris. In Seattle, reports Sarah Tyndal, a counselor with Pierce County Community Service, people with reverse mortgages have bought season tickets to Seattle Mariners baseball games for their whole family. But in less fortunate areas like Michigan, says Mike Gruley of First Financial Mortgage, perhaps one or two out of a hundred do.

In any case, frivolity is in the eye of the beholder. If someone is wealthy, why not take a little flier? I occasionally meet elderly people who are well heeled but timid about spending a dime. I tell them: Enjoy a night at the opera! Take some friends to the Four Seasons restaurant! Live it up a little!

Joseph DeMarkey recalls a borrower in the Northeast intent on becoming a snowbird. He used a lump sum reverse mortgage to buy a second home in Florida. Other borrowers have told him that they plan to take around-the-world cruises.

Sarah Hulbert says that most people use the money from reverse mortgages to pay off their existing mortgages and pressing bills, and in general to subsidize their retirement. But in one case, a mother was well-to-do, and so was her son. He didn't need money. So she obtained a reverse mortgage and, at his suggestion, went on an around-the-world cruise—for a full year. "She was 85 years old at the time, and she told me that the trip was fantastic."

John Curtis of Wells Fargo Home Mortgage closed a reverse mortgage for a 90-year-old man who wanted to buy a new car. According to Curtis, "He said, 'I want to get a PT Cruiser.' He wanted to do it because he had a girlfriend." Then there was the 90-year-old man in New Jersey who bought a Ferrari because, he explained, his 50-year-old girlfriend thought he looked good in it.

So, wealthy people do take out reverse mortgages?

Yes, because they, too, can have too much house and too little cash. Financial Freedom is a reverse-mortgage company in Irvine, California, that specializes in reverse mortgages for the wealthy (see Chapter 11).

Bill Agner tells of this unusual case: "Five or six years ago, the husband of an 80-year-old woman passed away. She owned a large property, and she tried to sell it but had no luck. She needed money to live on. So she got a reverse mortgage for $80,000 to $100,000, as I recall. A year later, she and her son came into my office. They had just sold the property and closed on it, for around $4 million. She paid off the mortgage. And then she hugged me and said, 'You saved my life.' I'll never forget that. But I was just doing my job."

Why are reverse mortgages so much in the news lately?

Many older people have not saved nearly enough for their retirement—"enough" is considered roughly 70 or 80 percent of their preretirement annual income.

This is especially true of Baby Boomers. They have saved little; many have not invested especially profitably with their 401(k) and other retirement plans.

Just as worrisome, Social Security benefits will surely be reduced in the future, or the age when people receive benefits will be pushed up again, or both. Meanwhile, health-care costs are expected to soar—at the same time that Medicare and Medicaid may be forced to become less generous. In short, the United States is clearly facing a retirement crisis.

One possible solution: encouraging homeowners to retire "on the house." To continue living in their houses, while borrowing money to live on—a loan, backed by their house, that they must eventually repay.

How is the U.S. government encouraging reverse mortgages?

An unsung genius at the Department of Housing and Urban Development came up with the idea of offering insurance for reverse mortgages—so that even if borrowers owed more than their house should ever sell for, the lender could not collect anything more. Another genius at HUD—maybe the same gifted person—decided that no one could obtain a home equity conversion mortgage (HECM, pronounced, "hecum"), HUD's own mortgage, without consulting an objective, well-informed counselor. Instead of a real estate agent, who might want homeowners to sell their houses and buy another one (two commissions) or a financial planner who might want homeowners to sell their houses and invest their profits (under the expensive guidance of the planner).

Joseph DeMarkey puts it this way: "The counselor, an objective third party, advises the homeowner about the suitability of the different products with respect to their needs, describes the costs involved, and dispels any incorrect information the client may have."

When must homeowners or their heirs repay the loan?

The loan must be repaid under the following circumstances:

1. The homeowners move out permanently (for 12 consecutive months).
2. They sell the home.
3. The last surviving borrower dies.

Must the house eventually be sold to repay the loan?

Not if the homeowners or their heirs have money to repay the loan, money apart from the sale of the house. Or if they refinance the loan into a traditional forward mortgage.

When will the bank's payments run out?

If the homeowner has chosen to receive monthly payments, the payments will never end as long as the homeowner lives there. Exception: if the homeowner has chosen a particular reverse mortgage that ends after, say, 10 years. This is a "term" instead of a "tenure" mortgage, and it is rare. A homeowner might do it because he or she is planning to sell another valuable asset in 10 years, like a boat, or start collecting Social Security in a few years.

Why do all reverse mortgages have adjustable rates— they go up with interest rates in general?

Thomas Scabareti, a mortgage authority, reports that HUD does permit fixed-rate mortgages, but the investors who eventually buy reverse mortgages for their portfolios want variable rates; they don't want to receive interest rates that may remain low when interest rates in general have climbed.

Is it true that you can use your reverse-mortgage money for anything? Anything legal, that is?

No. You cannot use the loan to pay anyone at all for having given you advice about a reverse mortgage. Scabareti reports that only a HUD-approved lender or a licensed mortgage broker working with a HUD-approved lender can receive compensation for the origination of a loan.

Can I be turned down for a reverse mortgage? If, for example, my house is a dump?

Yes. A house must be inspected, and if a lot of repair work is needed, you may not qualify. HUD lets you obtain a reverse mortgage if the repairs are estimated to be 15 percent or less of the maximum principal limit that you would otherwise qualify for. If the repairs are between 15 percent and 30 percent, the borrower can have enough repairs done to bring the amount down to 15 percent and then finalize the loan. If the repairs amount to over 30 percent, no loan.

If you have a pending lawsuit or are in bankruptcy, you may also be denied the loan. And Scabareti points out that if you have too large a mortgage against your house, you may also be turned down. But if you can get outside funds—from a relative, for example—to help pay off the mortgage at the closing, the loan could go forward, as long as the new loan is in the first-loan position.

I would like to tear down my house and build another. Can I get a reverse mortgage and use the money to build a new house?

No. You could get a reverse mortgage and use the money to build a second home, but if you tear down the primary residence, the loan is due and payable.

Besides, currently HUD prohibits a reverse mortgage on homes that are less than one year old, so you would have to wait to do a reverse mortgage on the new home.

It's a "reverse" mortgage because the bank pays you?

Yes. In a traditional or "forward" mortgage, you typically make a down payment and then regularly pay the lender for the money advanced to you, along with interest. In a reverse mortgage, the bank may pay you a monthly income for as long as you live in the house. Or you may choose to receive a lump sum, or obtain a line of credit, or choose a combination of ways to receive the loan. So a reverse mortgage is not quite the mirror image of a forward mortgage.

What choices do I have?

You can receive a lump sum, a line of credit, a monthly income, or a combination of these. Most people choose a line of credit, which may be the most sensible.

Where do I get a reverse mortgage?

You begin with an "originator," who completes the paperwork.

Will I have to pay anything?

Yes, the closing costs, as with any mortgage.

What if I don't have enough cash to pay even the closing costs?

They can be folded into the loan, so you will have few or no out-of-pocket expenses.

Can two people who are not married, but own a house together, get a reverse mortgage? This might include brothers and sisters or domestic partners.

Yes.

What should I do with the money?

First, you must pay off any mortgage you already have and make any needed repairs to your home. Then you should pay off any credit card bills you may have, because of their high interest rates. Pay off other bills, too. Next, develop a plan (see Chapter 15).

What should I not do?

In general, don't get a reverse mortgage if you suspect you will live in your house for only a few years. If, for example, you are planning to move to a smaller home in a warmer climate soon, or your health is such that you are thinking of moving to an assisted-living facility. The closing costs will come back and bite you.

"You can't predict these things," says Mike Gruley (president of First Financial Mortgage Corp.) sensibly. "You must plan as best you can. But even if you live in your house a short time, for one or two years, it's not devastating. It's expensive, but it's not the end of the world. And if you proceed to live in your home for your life expectancy—20 or 30 years, say— the cost of the loan will have been quite low."

As always, there are exceptions. Bill Agner (director of reverse mortgages for the Mortgage Network in Indianapolis) tells of one of the first reverse mortgages he ever arranged—for a 103-year-old man. He had lived in his home for 60 or 70 years, was in poor health now, and needed money for caregivers. He knew that he had only a short time to live, but he wanted to remain in his home. He obtained a $50,000 reverse mortgage, which provided him with money to live on and to pay for special care. He died a year and a half later—in his home.

Don't go haywire because of all that ready money. Don't succumb to lottery-winner syndrome and start spending like mad. Neale Godfrey, a best-selling author, tells of six grandchildren who inherited $20 million each. Within 18 months, each of them had gone through all that money, having invested it in such projects as fitness centers which they knew nothing about.

Don't become a victim of the crooks and quasi-crooks out there, eager to part you from your money. Beware of people trying to sell you small-company stocks, commodities, deferred annuities, life insurance, or miraculous life-prolonging medications that the medical profession in a cruel conspiracy wants to keep you from using.

Never buy anything over the phone. Do what I do: "Good evening, Warren. And how are you this evening, Warren?" "Busy!" (Sound of phone slamming down.) See Chapter 16.

Can I get a reverse mortgage on my summer home?
No, it must be your main residence.

What kinds of residences don't qualify?
Motor homes and cooperatives (except co-ops in New York state, which do qualify).

Can I have a mortgage on my house and still get a reverse mortgage?

Only if your mortgage is small enough to be paid off by the reverse mortgage.

A man is 62, but his wife is 58. Can they still get a reverse mortgage?

Only the person aged 62 can—if his spouse is no longer a co-owner and her name is removed from the title to the house. But in that case, if the older person died, the loan would become due and the house might have to be sold—perhaps something that the spouse wouldn't want.

A couple like that might be better off waiting four years before applying for a reverse mortgage.

In case there is a wide difference in ages, the older homeowner might buy a term insurance policy, with the spouse as the beneficiary. If the older homeowner dies first, the survivor can use the money from the insurance to pay off the loan, thus keeping the house. This is one of the rare instances in which older people might consider purchasing life insurance.

Thomas Scabareti knows of a mother, 90, and her daughter, 72, who obtained a reverse mortgage together. If the mother had taken her daughter off the title, in order to obtain a bigger loan, there might have been trouble. Even if the daughter inherited the house, probate court proceedings might have taken a long time. The same goes for taking a spouse off the title—it's perilous. Talk to a lawyer first.

Okay, what's wrong with reverse mortgages?

The closing costs are high, for one thing. Especially if you live in the house for a short time after getting such a mortgage.

Where can I get objective advice? Should I go to a financial planner?

I admire financial planners, especially certified financial planners, especially certified financial planners who charge fees and not commissions, especially such planners who belong to the National Association of Personal Financial Advisors (see Chapter 7).

Financial planners can be helpful in checking your entire financial situation—your investments, your taxes, your will, your insurance. But some of them seem prejudiced against reverse mortgages. And some may be tempted to persuade homeowners to sell their houses, so that they can manage all the money the ex-homeowners receive.

In any case, to obtain any reverse mortgage at all, you must consult with a reverse mortgage counselor approved by HUD. And HUD won't let you use proceeds from a reverse mortgage to pay anyone for advice about getting a reverse mortgage except counselors it has approved.

Should I go to a real-estate broker for guidance?

Brokers can be helpful, but they may be tempted to persuade homeowners to sell their houses and move to smaller houses nearby, with the result that the brokers collect two commissions. This may actually be a wise step on the part of the homeowners, but it's better that such advice come from someone disinterested, like a reverse mortgage counselor.

What if the monthly income from my reverse mortgage isn't enough?

You can change your payment to a larger monthly income. Or you can get a one-time lump sum, along with the monthly income. Contact the loan servicer to ask that the loan be "modified." Maybe your monthly income will be reduced so you will get that lump sum. Modifications typically cost $20.

If your lender's loan limits have increased, you can also refinance the loan to boost the funds you have available.

I wanted to leave the house to my kids. Will I be able to if I get a reverse mortgage?

If you live a very long time while collecting a monthly income and the house doesn't appreciate much if at all, your heirs may receive very little. But in all likelihood there will be some profit.

Should I tell my kids about the reverse mortgage?

In general, yes, so that they can give you advice. So that they won't suspect that you are being taken advantage of. And so that if you ever have another tough decision to make, you will normally think of talking to them first.

What if I change my mind?

You have three business days from the day you sign the contract to change your mind. (Saturdays are included, but not Sundays or holidays.)

*Are there things I might do that are better than
getting a reverse mortgage?*

See Chapter 5. But some other possibilities include

1. Selling your house to your children in return for lifetime income.
2. Refinancing your mortgage.
3. Getting a home-equity loan.
4. Getting a home-equity loan, and using it to purchase an income annuity. (*Not* a deferred annuity—see Chapter 16.)
5. Selling your house and moving to a smaller, less expensive house or a less expensive community. Or renting.
6. Reducing your standard of living.
7. Continuing to work or—if you were retired—getting a new job.

You could combine some of these alternatives with a reverse mortgage. You could, for example, sell your house, move to a less expensive house, then get a reverse mortgage on that new house. And you could lower your expenditures (item 6) and continue working (item 7) at the same time.

*What if I marry someone who, like me, already has
a house with a reverse mortgage?*

You might want to pay off both of your loans and obtain a new reverse mortgage together on one of the houses.

If just one spouse pays off the loan and moves in with the other, the mortgage becomes due when the homeowner dies, even if the spouse is still living in the house.

What if a couple with a reverse mortgage gets divorced?

If one spouse moves out, the mortgage remains in force until the other spouse moves out permanently or dies.

*What if I decide to spend a year in France. Will my
reverse mortgage remain in effect?*

If you are gone for over a year, the loan becomes due.

May I rent out my home?

You may, but, unless it is your own main home, the loan will become due.

Exhibit 1.1 lists 12 reasons to consider getting a reverse mortgage.

Exhibit 1.1 Top 12 Reasons to Consider a Reverse Mortgage

12. You can continue to live in your house. You need not move to a new place where you might have to find a new doctor, a new barber/beautician, a new accountant, a new lawyer, a new stockbroker, new friends. Along with new restaurants, new stores, new garage mechanics. You also won't have to learn new routes, new streets, new shortcuts.

11. You can receive cash—to pay your bills, to improve your lifestyle. More meals out; more shows; more trips; new, better clothes. You may be able to afford gifts for your children and grandchildren.

10. To qualify—no income levels, no minimum credit score, no minimum assets, no medical tests. (But you cannot have large debts apart from a reasonable mortgage on your house.)

9. You can decide in what form to receive your money. A lump sum to pay debts? A monthly income for as long as you live in the house? A line of credit so that you never have to pay interest on any money unless you withdraw it? A combination of these choices?

8. You need not make any payments until the home is no longer your principal residence.

7. The money is untaxed.

6. You can get free—or at least inexpensive—advice from an informed, objective source: a HUD-approved counselor. There are other protections for the borrower, too—interest rates have lifetime limits on them, you get three business days to change your mind, you are told in advance what the closing costs may be, there is no prepayment penalty, and the government guarantees that you will receive your money.

5. With the most popular type of reverse mortgage, the HECM, your credit line automatically goes up.

4. You or your heirs don't ever have to sell the house. You or your heirs can use other assets to pay off your debt.

3. You can diversify your portfolio. If most of your wealth was in your house, putting a little of your equity into stocks and bonds makes sense.

Exhibit 1.1 (*Continued*)

> 2. You can use the money for almost whatever you want. To pay off your mortgage, to take an around-the-world tour. It's your money.
> 1. Even if the value of the house turns out to be less than the money you borrowed, neither you nor your heirs will owe the bank a penny. A reverse mortgage is a "nonrecourse" loan.

Table 1.1 concisely summarizes the difference between traditional mortgages and reverse mortgages.

Table 1.1 Traditional vs. Reverse Mortgage

	Traditional (Forward)	Reverse
Reason for loan:	To buy a house	To get income
Equity in home:	Little	Great deal
During loan:	Makes payments	May receive payments
	Loan balance goes down	Loan balance may climb
	Deducts interest	Normally does not deduct interest
At end of loan:	Owes nothing	Owes not more than house value
	Owns house	Has less equity

2

Real People Talk about Their Reverse Mortgages

People who have obtained reverse mortgages tend to use a single word: *godsend*.

Of course, these people were not part of a scientific survey. Their names in many cases were obtained from men and women in the reverse-mortgage industry, so they are a selected sample—selected, no doubt, in part because of their happy experiences. Besides, once you do something, you tend to want to believe that you did the right thing. People who bet on a horse at the track tend to be more optimistic about their choice after rather than before they made the bet.

Even so, the satisfaction of most of these people is hard to ignore. Besides, counselors who deal with borrowers keep telling me, sincerely, how much a reverse mortgage has improved people's lives. "A lot of seniors," reports Mike Gruley of First Financial Mortgage in Northville, Michigan, "are just getting by. They live on an $800 pension check and Social Security. Then the furnace needs fixing, or the roof needs repairing, or there are medical costs or property taxes. These $1,000 or $2,000 bills blow their budgets out.

"I keep getting letters, and cards, from people who tell me how much a reverse mortgage changed their lives, how it improved the quality of their lives. It's such a pleasure."

Says Isis Malagrino, a counselor with Novadebt in Fairhold, New Jersey, "It's a good feeling when you're doing what's right for them, and when they call back and tell you that they're now happy and living comfortably again. It's a very rewarding job."

Patricia: *"The best deal going for senior citizens."*

The house of Patricia Thomas, 63, who lives in the Detroit area, was "ready to fall down." Among other things, it needed a new roof and a new furnace. She could not afford them. She tried to refinance her mortgage, but she was turned down because her credit score was too low.

When she learned about reverse mortgages, she said, "My goodness!" Now she is glad she didn't refinance.

Her counselor was "excellent." The originator was First Financial Mortgage. She chose the credit line. "When I need extra money, I send for it," she says. "The check is in my hand in five days." Even after paying off her previous mortgage and having her house repaired, she still has money left.

She started the process two months before she turned 62.

"Equity was just sitting there, and here was a chance to use it. Now my house is looking good. I would do nothing differently." She was not planning to leave her house to her children.

"This is the best thing that ever happened to poor people."

John: *"No regrets."*

John L. Butler, 70, of Ridgewood, New Jersey, is a retired consultant of technical documentation for securities firms and, recently, a tax preparer for H&R Block. He remains busy, playing an above-average game of tennis, painting (mainly sailing ships), and chairing a book club whose members read books like *King Leopold's Ghost* by Adam Hochschild and the Civil War stories of Ambrose Bierce.

He was in the process of obtaining a reverse mortgage in 2005 because he was pleased with the notion of receiving tax-free income (a reverse mortgage is just a loan) and because he wanted to buy long-term care insurance for himself and his wife, Louise. (They wound up buying a John Hancock policy, for $5,700 a year, which he decided after diligent research was a bargain.) He receives Social Security payments and has some money in securities, but no pension.

What he has is a house that is worth a lot of money. Ridgewood is an upscale community filled with business executives and professionals, along with expensive restaurants—and with its own Gilbert & Sullivan operetta company. He bought his house in 1998, and the price proceeded to soar. "I'm embarrassed to tell you how much I made," he said with a smile.

He studied information about reverse mortgages on the AARP Web site, checked how much he might borrow with such a mortgage, and obtained the names of mortgage originators. His house had been appraised at $595,000, and he could obtain a reverse mortgage based on a limit of $312,895, the maximum HECM loan insured by the FHA for homeowners in his area at the time.

Why didn't he move to, say, South Carolina, where the cost of living might have been lower? "We're well established here," he replied. They like the area and their home. Mrs. Butler, a violin teacher, has students here. "We have no reason to move."

In fact, five years ago they added an extra bedroom and bath to their house, and, now, if either of them needs home care, there's that room.

What about selling his house to his children, in return for an annuity? No, the children would then have to be responsible for the taxes, for the repairs, plus supporting the parents. "The complications would have been too much," says John.

Why not just a home-equity loan, with its low or nonexistent closing costs? "We didn't want to be responsible for monthly payments."

He phoned an AARP counselor, Amy Pinto, and made a phone reservation two weeks from that time. She was ready when his wife Louise called. Butler spoke with Pinto for 50 minutes. Pinto was well prepared, conscientious, and well organized. She explained matters, answered questions, and even asked some of her own. What would they do with the money? Do they plan to stay there? "She was easy to understand," he said. "And she didn't rush us."

"My biggest concern," Butler went on, "was verifying that my children had no contingent liability—that if I died and the house was worth less than the loan, they would not have to make up the difference." He also confirmed that if one of the spouses died, the other could continue to live in the house and receive monthly payments.

The very next day, the Butlers received their certification in the mail.

Two mortgage specialists from different originators came to his home. One, from a national company, didn't make an especially good impression. He seemed to think that just because his office was nearby, that was a big advantage. (Butler didn't want to identify the company.) The other specialist, from a local company called Amston Mortgage, was more "professional."

In checking out the New Jersey originators online, Butler had found something interesting. One well-known bank would charge $5,100 as an origination fee, instead of the maximum 2 percent that HUD permits—$6,258. (He also didn't want to identify the bank.)

Butler mentioned that to the Amston specialist. Okay, he would come down all the way to $4,500. Informed of this, the other big player's specialist also offered to retreat to $4,500. "You're eating into my commission," he complained. When Butler told that to Amston, its representative responded that, just to break the tie, he would go down to $4,400.

An appraisal, taking a half hour, cost $450, which could not be financed with the loan and had to be paid up front. One problem: Butler had to fix a leaking underground oil tank, a problem that is almost epidemic in that area.

All in all, the cost was almost $14,000 (see Exhibit 2.1). Of the $312,895 maximum, he was able to borrow around 70 percent, which amounted to $218,400. Butler chose the monthly-income option, not the lump sum or the line of credit.

His advice to others: Do a lot of research beforehand, using the Internet if you can. And if you feel you owe your kids your house and you don't really need any extra money, maybe you shouldn't get a reverse mortgage.

Stew and Margie: *"It's allowed us to do all kinds of things."*

This was Stew Brown's second reverse mortgage. The first one, in 1997, paid for his daughter's wedding. Since then, his first wife, Sharon, died. Stew, who turned 75 in 2005, remarried. His new wife, Margie, 69, had

Exhibit 2.1 John Butler's Closing Costs

The following costs are taken from the "good faith estimate" supplied by Amston Mortgage Co., rounded to the nearest dollar.	
Loan origination fee	$4,400
Credit report	19
Repair administration fee	50
Flood certification fee	20
FHA mortgage insurance	6,258
Closing fee	350
Title insurance	1,382
Endorsements	350
Recording fee	350
Pest inspection fee	95
Appraisal	450
Total	$13,724

been a widow. Together they applied for a second reverse mortgage, a HECM, and chose a lump sum. They live on Vashon Island in Washington.

They used some of the money to take a cruise to Alaska. Some of the remainder went to pay for Stew's prescriptions—he has had cancer for some time. Recently his cancer was diagnosed as especially serious.

Says Lee McCutcheon of Seattle Mortgage, "He is probably the most positive, upbeat, wonderful person I have worked with in all my years in the business."

Stew, when asked why he obtained such a mortgage, replied, "For financial security. It allows us to do things that otherwise we wouldn't be able to do—like travel. We've gone to the Palm Desert in California, taken an Alaska cruise—that was phenomenal. It's allowed us to do all kinds of things. To improve our house—we had it all painted and updated everything. We paid off around $12,000 in credit card debt. We can't say often enough how much this has meant to us."

When he applied for the mortgage, he did not know he had cancer, and the money he received has also helped defray the cost of expensive cancer medications. "They told me," he said, "that so far they can't identify the cancer, but it's incurable. I said that that word is not in my vocabulary."

For a time he couldn't even walk, but with radiation therapy to shrink the mass of cancer on his spine, he now has complete mobility. He's also completely pain-free. "So now, with the reverse money, we can do some other things. It has allowed us to live without having any concern about money, concerns that make you sit back and wish you could afford to do things."

Vashon Island is in the middle of Puget Sound, between Seattle and Tacoma. The island is reachable only by ferry. Stew has owned the house for 39 years, and has lived there steadily for 13 years.

Before retiring he was a sales manager, whereas Margie was a teacher, and she retired from teaching just last year. "When you teach middle school," he said about her retirement, "you need all the vim and vigor you've got."

Did he consider a home-equity loan? An income annuity? "The only one that interested me was a reverse mortgage," he answered. "I liked the fact that I can live in the house as long as I want and there's nothing to pay. My kids will have a year in which to pay off the reverse mortgage, and then the place is theirs. I was able to swing it because this is waterfront property, and it has just accelerated in value. I've known Lee McCutcheon for eight or nine years, and he has just been there for us. He laid everything out, so we knew exactly what we were getting. He came over to close the deal for us."

Stew has four children, Margie has two, and they have eight grandchildren. How do their children feel about the mortgage? "They love it. They like to see us doing things."

Eva: *She told her son, "It's my house."*

Eva Heath of Salisbury, New Hampshire, is 78, a housewife, and a grandmother.

Her husband died six years ago, and now her 23-year-old grandson lives with her. She has lived in her Sears, Roebuck mail-order house for 40 years, and recently she needed some money to make some repairs and updates.

A reverse-mortgage counselor came to her senior center and gave a talk about reverse mortgages. "It sounded too good to be true," she said. "I told them it sounds good. Sign me up."

Eva chose a line of credit because she didn't need a whole lot of money. When she needs to pay another bill, her granddaughter faxes the lender, who puts money into her checking account. Eva paid for a new roof, siding, and windows; she replaced her floor, moved her sump pump, and had her septic system tank emptied. Soon she will be getting new electrical wiring for her house.

At one point, Eva almost didn't go through with it. "It seemed too good to be true," she explained, and she was worried that something would go wrong. But her counselor helped her see that she needn't worry. "I threatened to take all the paperwork and just walk out of there," Eva said with a laugh.

Her son had some reservations about the reverse mortgage. "I told him, 'It's my house,'" said Eva. "I explained that he would only have to pay back what I use, and I'm not using a lot."

Dorothy: *Still working at 80.*

At the age of 80, Dorothy Poplawski, a widow, was still teaching. She said, "I couldn't see how I could retire. Then I got a reverse mortgage, and I retired the next year."

"I was teaching preschool and sitting on a house worth money."

"I loved teaching and could have done it longer, but it's nice not to have to run out every morning."

She had been a teacher for 45 years, always preschool. She has lived all of her life in Seattle. Her husband died in 1952, when she was 23, pregnant, and with an 11-month-old son.

Did she consider any alternatives? "I didn't want to leave my house. But I guess I could have rented rooms out."

Her son, 53, now a park ranger in Steamboat Road, Washington, suggested the reverse mortgage. She obtained a HECM from Financial Freedom, choosing a line of credit. She gets $600 a month from the mortgage and another $600 from Social Security.

"I've told two other people about reverse mortgages, and they've gotten them, too."

The lenders checked her house, built in 1911, and asked that the roof be repaired, the front porch painted, and railings added. These repairs came off the top of the loan.

Have there been any changes in her life?

"No. Just busy as ever. I volunteer as historian at a West Seattle high school alumni group. I go there one day a week. Across the street from my house is a park, one of the first city parks in the country. I'm writing a history of the park. I do that one day a week."

Bruce: *"It made some dreams come true."*

A retired manager at General Electric, Bruce Carter of Boxford, Massachusetts, was surprised to learn a few years ago that there was such a thing as a reverse mortgage. Yet his own reverse mortgage has helped "make some dreams come true."

Before getting one, he was able to pay his bills—but he was not able to buy "quality things."

One thing he did with the money: He and his wife and one of their sons, a biologist, went on a trip to Africa. "It was the trip of a lifetime," he said happily. They also visited South America and traveled up the Amazon, and just returned from a trip to Russia.

With the money, he was even able to help out his three sons financially. "We got to see the enjoyment of our sons while we were still alive." They even had some money left over to improve their house. They never thought of selling. They like their house too much.

Yes, they considered alternatives, but "none were as good. Our reverse mortgage has certainly improved the Carter family's life."

They had their house built in 1974 for $45,000. Not long ago it was appraised at almost $600,000. Of the mortgage, he said: "I thought I'd never pay it off."

They obtained the mortgage through the Bank of New York and chose a line of credit, Other people he knows had done that. Recently he refinanced, so he has an even larger line of credit.

Any problems, any drawbacks? "I kept waiting for the other shoe to fall, but it didn't. These are the good old days."

Jim: *Around the world in two months.*

Jim Tulare of Graham, Washington, obtained a reverse mortgage. Then he and his wife took a two-month trip around the world.

"I have a lot of equity in my house, and I didn't want to be infirm before I had a chance to use it," he said. "I wanted to enjoy life more.

They started out in New Zealand and then went to Sydney and the east coast of Australia, where they hopped a train. In Perth they visited a lot of vineyards, and then they went on to Frankfurt. Next, they boarded *Windstar,* a cruise ship with 148 passengers and an 88-member crew. "We sailed around the Greek islands, then on to Athens and then home."

On the trip, they met someone who asked them: Are you "SKI" people? Meaning: spending the kids' inheritance.

Obviously, the Tulares are not house-rich and cash-poor, a common situation for people who obtain reverse mortgages. Instead of spending down their securities, they decided to spend down the equity in their house.

"We have a fair amount of money in stocks and bonds," Tulare said. "We have Social Security, a pension, good medical insurance. We're active. If you've got your health, you've got everything. We raise a glass every day and toast our lives."

Tulare had been talking with Lee McCutcheon about reverse mortgages for two or three years. Then, over a year ago, the couple told him they were seriously interested. It took a month or two to work out the details. The house had to be inspected. They had to have counseling. McCutcheon "made sure we knew what we were getting into and the costs. He was very professional."

They obtained a line of credit. "We didn't need the money to pay any bills." The reverse mortgage covered their existing mortgage, so they no longer had payments to make. He didn't know whether it was a HECM or not.

What did their kids think about the trip? "They approved of it. We set up a Web site and e-mailed back and forth—nine or ten messages a week."

As a hobby, Tulare and his wife run a vineyard; they made 22 cases of wine this year, with grapes from eastern Washington. He has had the vineyard for 15 years. "A labor-intensive hobby," he calls it. "It takes a year to make one bottle of wine." Before that, he worked for 3M as a salesman for nearly 25 years before retiring. He turned 70 in 2005.

He had told their three children that he and his wife were checking into a reverse mortgage. "One disagreed with the move, and the other two didn't care. The one that disagreed was in real estate."

With the extra money the couple also bought new furniture and put a new roof on house. He's changing his wood-burning stove to propane so he doesn't have to chop wood anymore. They are planning another trip, to Norway, where their families came from. They will also go to Scotland, Italy, Austria, and Switzerland.

Did he feel he wanted to leave their kids some money? "If they get a nickel, it's too much," he said with a laugh. "They don't want it. They're all professional people."

Do they have an e-mail address? "No. I threw the computer out the window when I retired."

Bill: *"I decided to enjoy myself for the time I have."*

Bill Wagar of Livonia, Michigan, thought about a reverse mortgage because in 2005 he wanted money to attend the 50th reunion of U.S. soldiers who had participated in the invasion of Normandy in 1945. But his wife, who had been ill, died, and he did not feel like going.

He decided to take a trip after she died. "I didn't have enough cash, so I decided to take this reverse mortgage and see how it works." He turned 83 in 2005, and "I decided to enjoy myself for the time I have."

He will be going to Normandy in the spring of 2006. He is going with a friend, and they will probably visit Paris, Rome, and Spain, places he visited during World War II.

A former manager of fleet and government sales for General Motors, Wagar retired in 1985. He has lived in Livonia for 41 years. He has four children—two boys, two girls. He spoke to them. Two said, "Do what you want to do. Spend it all." One son didn't comment, and his youngest daughter had some reservations.

He read up on the subject and then met with a counselor. "The counselor was not very thorough," said Wagar, "but I understood it on my own. I had two or three questions, and the counselor seemed shocked that I didn't have more."

He obtained a HECM, and a credit line—because "You're only paying interest for the money you use. If the interest goes too high, I'm going to pay it off and forget it."

Any drawbacks? "No, I'm happy with it."

Any changes in his life as a result of the mortgage? No. "I've used some of the money to do things around the house—new driveway, new security fence. I was going to do those anyway."

Susan: *"It was a godsend."*

Susan Iapicca of West Orange, New Jersey, had what she calls a streak of bad luck. She owns a two-family house in a working-class town, and tenant after tenant declined to pay the rent. And without that rent, she couldn't pay her own mortgage.

"I couldn't keep up," she said. "I was worried about bills. I was frantic. Would I be foreclosed? Put out of my home?" A retired nurse, she was 72 when I interviewed her in 2005.

She has two grandchildren living with her, ages 16 and 12. Her daughter-in-law had left her son; her son now lives with Susan's ex-husband not far away.

She had received phone calls from salespeople urging her to refinance her existing mortgage. They talked about credit and interest rates, but "No one gives you any numbers to work with. I was stressed out—everyone was taking advantage. I had lots of headaches and never could get a decent night's sleep." Sometimes she would ask the telemarketers for an interest rate and never hear from them again. "It was a merry-go-round. I was between a rock and a hard place."

One tenant told her he was a car salesman, but "He paid in dribs and drabs." His excuse: Cars weren't selling that month.

To replace him, she was considering a man whose wife was a consultant to the public schools. The two saw the rooms together, and the wife said she loved it. He gave Susan a check for $2,450 for security. "He seemed okay. Nice."

Then she tried phoning him, but the number wasn't working. And all he had was a cell phone. So she visited his residence and by chance spoke to a mailman and a neighbor. The couple was always moving, she learned. And not paying rent.

She had not cashed the security check. She phoned the bank. "There was zero balance. Such manipulators!"

She spoke to a social worker, who referred her to a reverse-mortgage specialist with Wells Fargo in Paramus, New Jersey. She cannot praise him enough.

Later she spoke to a HUD counselor, David M. Stevens in Newark, and signed a reverse-mortgage contract with Wells Fargo. "They're good people," she said. "I had been skeptical. The bank doesn't own your house. I thought they take your house if you pass [on]. But if you paid it back, fine."

"If not for the reverse mortgage," she went on, "I don't know what I would have done." She added, "It's only for seniors!"

"It was a godsend," she said. "What would I have done? I'm so happy with the contract. I sleep peacefully now. It was a blessing."

Her house was appraised at $350,000. She took a lump sum to pay $4,000 of her car loan, as well as money to have her house repainted as was required by the terms of the loan. She had $80,000 left as a line of credit, and whenever she needs money, she calls Wells Fargo to move money into her account.

She is planning to re-rent the apartment, and she intends to pay back the reverse mortgage. "There are always ways to make money," she said brightly. And: "I pray all the time. God is good."

Mary: *"Outrageous."*

Mary (not her real name) is a retired banker and is knowledgeable about mortgages. She applied for a reverse mortgage, and then turned it down. "Outrageous" is the word she uses again and again.

What she objected to were the closing costs.

"A $5,000 origination fee! A courier! These fees are outrageous!" The total for the closing costs would have been $13,763. "That would have supported me for a lot of months."

She owns a $400,000 house. She was thinking that some extra money might help if she ever needed home health care, which might cost $3,000 a month. And she was curious about reverse mortgages. "I have an inquisitive mind."

She's not needy. "I have enough. I've done fairly well. I own mainly stocks. I made a good salary as a banker. At one time, I had three jobs at once. I've had a sad but interesting life." (She was divorced a long time ago.)

But she's energetic and good-natured. "Bankers never die," she told me, repeating an old joke. "We just lose interest."

She has a sister in North Carolina who wants her to live with her. "But I have nothing there. I have friends here."

Mary's aversion to those newfangled reverse mortgages is understandable, even though I disagree with her. Paying $13,000 all at once may seem outrageous, which is why people seeking reverse mortgages should plan to live in their homes for at least three years.

Recently Mary met someone in a supermarket, who, knowing she was a mortgage expert, asked her about reverse mortgages. "Get a home-equity loan instead," she told him. "No outrageous closing costs."

Paul: "It's worked out pretty good."

A former Linotype operator for *The Record,* a daily newspaper in New Jersey, Paul Zitelli is 87. His wife, 78, had a stroke a while back and spent almost two years in a nursing home. When she was discharged, Paul had to renovate his home in Bergenfield to accommodate her—installing chairlifts, for example.

"I used up my reserve funds. All I had left was Social Security."

He consulted a social worker, and "a pleasant lady" suggested that he consider a reverse mortgage. He dealt with Wells Fargo, and "It's worked out pretty good."

His home is a split-level with three bedrooms and one and a half baths. When he was told that it was worth $400,000, he said, "Wow! That's a lot!"

From the reverse mortgage he gets regular monthly payments, which pay for nurses' aides, who, besides everything else they do, clean and cook. Medicaid picks up the medical bills and the cost of prescriptions.

"Wells Fargo told me that I could do anything I want with the money," he said admiringly. "And if I want more or need more, they can advance that, too—above what they already send me.

"I'm very happy with it. No problems at all.

"My children were in on it. I have six children. They thought it was a good idea. They came with me when the lady covered it.

"It's worked out fine. But it will run out."

I told him that the payments wouldn't run out. I was surprised that he didn't understand this.

"Will it last me all my life? Ten years is all I want—if I live that long. We'll talk about it then."

Caryl: *"The fees were a real shock."*

Caryl Derryberry, 75, of Lakewood, Colorado, a retired antiques dealer, came down with pneumonia and then had trouble paying her bills. All she was living on was a Social Security check. A reverse mortgage helped out. She even was able to replace a defective air conditioner and furnace.

"I do not know what else I would have done, outside of selling my condo outright, and then I would still have had to find a place to live," she told Jeffrey Brown of the *Denver Post* (July 24, 2005). "This was a godsend, as far as I am concerned, once it was explained to me."

She added: "The fees were a real shock, and I am not over it yet."

Ruth: *"Money to make us comfortable."*

Peter and Ruth Ricca of Metairie, Louisiana, obtained a reverse mortgage to "give us a pad, an extra bit of money to make us comfortable." She was 78 and her husband, Peter, was 80. Up to that point, they had only their Social Security and their savings to live on.

They had retired from the grocery and restaurant business 14 years before. Their house was valued at $230,000, and they received a lump-sum payment of $105,000. Some $15,000 paid off a bank loan, and $15,000 paid off other bills. They are keeping the remaining $75,000.

Said Mrs. Ricca, "We're very happy with the arrangement." (From *Retire on Less Than You Think*, by Fred Brock, Times Books, 2004.)

Aleck: *"I want to spend my last dime."*

Aleck and Sheila Townsley of Forster City, California, are well-to-do; he is a retired lawyer, she is a retired teacher. In 1999, when they were both 65, they obtained a reverse mortgage on their $555,000 house, choosing a $65,000 line of credit. Reason: so they could afford "extras" like traveling.

Said Aleck, "We have no children. I want to spend my last dime with my last breath."

Stephen and Gladys: *"One of the greatest things."*

"We were getting along in years, and reverse mortgages are one of the greatest things that can happen to someone getting old," said Gladys Cullen, 82, of Oxford, Massachusetts.

"We just wanted a little more cash to fix up the house," added her husband Stephen, 88, a retired accountant. They had a lot of money left even outside their home. "And nobody can touch that," said Stephen, "because it's a nonrecourse loan."

Their counselors were "very, very good people."

Any drawbacks, any problems? "No drawbacks whatsoever that I know of. We've been very pleased with it. It gives us cash to live on." They had obtained a line of credit from the Bank of New York. What about their children—how do they feel about it? "They feel great. They didn't want our property, and they're well off themselves."

3

Those Scary Stories You May Have Heard

Reverse mortgages are such a neat and reasonable solution to the money problems of certain older people that it's weird how much misinformation has been circulating out there about them, and how much hostility the idea has received from people who should know better. (See Exhibit 3.1.)

The most common misinformation: Homeowners will lose their houses. A bank will become the new owner. The homeowner, in his or her old, old age, will be wind up being evicted.

Yet if just one borrower with a reverse mortgage were ever to be forcibly evicted, it might make newspaper headlines all over the country, and the entire concept of a reverse mortgage, so enthusiastically endorsed by the U.S. government via the Department of Housing and Urban Affairs and by AARP, would be tarnished.

Yet it might happen. Here is one scenario: An elderly homeowner, with no one to help him or her, becomes irreversibly incapacitated. The homeowner stops paying property taxes and home insurance. The lawn

Exhibit 3.1 Myths about Reverse Mortgages

> *Myth:* The bank will own the home.
> *Reality:* The borrower continues to retain title and ownership.
>
> *Myth:* The heirs will be stuck with repaying the loan.
> *Reality:* The estate is protected from ever owing more than the value of the home. The reverse mortgage is a nonrecourse loan.
>
> *Myth:* Reverse mortgages will affect Social Security and Medicare payments.
> *Reality:* Because the loan proceeds are not taxable, they do not raise your taxable income. So they do not affect Social Security or Medicare payments. (But they may affect Medicaid and other entitlement programs.)
>
> *Myth:* A senior must be in good health to qualify.
> *Reality:* There are no health requirements—and no income, asset, employment, or credit-score requirements.

needs mowing, the roof is leaking, windows are broken. At this point, a bank might go to court to order the homeowner to be transferred to a nursing home and the house sold to pay off the reverse mortgage. This seems justifiable. This might happen with a traditional mortgage, too. But typically what a lender does is reduce the monthly payments to pay off the debts.

Some of this misinformation about reverse mortgages may stem from the early days of such mortgages, when a few greedy lenders insisted on grabbing a huge slice of any profits if a senior's house grew in value. (They were called "shared appreciation mortgages.") There was thus a temptation for lenders to see to it that these houses were appraised at unrealistically low amounts because a lender profits more if a house is originally appraised at $200,000 rather than $250,000.

Some of the misconceptions about reverse mortgages may have been spread by a few real estate agents who were eager to cajole older home-owners into selling their houses and moving to something smaller and cheaper. This is sometimes a perfectly sensible step. (See Chapter 5.)

But the agent giving the guidance may not be a disinterested source. If the homeowner listens to the agent, the agent could wind up with two commissions.

As for financial planners, some of them are worried about reverse mortgages; others are simply dubious.

A certified financial planner (CFP), Steven Kaye of the American Economic Planning Group in Watchung, New Jersey, predicts, "They will be increasingly abused as the public becomes more aware of them as a resource to be tapped. They should be used in dire cases, but will be used by some irresponsibly—similar to people borrowing the cash value on their life insurance policies and diminishing or destroying their benefits."

Claire Toth, a lawyer and CFP in Springfield, New Jersey, is also worried. While she grants that for some seniors a reverse mortgage "may provide an answer to the cash crunch," she adds, "The only people for whom a reverse mortgage really makes any sense are those who have no other options."

Her objections:

1. *There are limits on how much you can borrow.* A 65-year-old in New Jersey could obtain $165,000. "That's hardly a windfall." (Actually, much more is available with a Financial Freedom reverse mortgage, not a HECM.)
2. *Not all homes qualify.* A home must have little or no mortgage debt and be in good repair. Generally you cannot get a reverse mortgage on a vacation home, a multifamily home with four or more units, or a manufactured home not permanently attached to a foundation.
3. *There are "hefty fees" involved.* Expect to pay at least 2 percent of the house's value, plus another 0.5 percent a month, if the mortgage is insured. On top of this there are mortgage application costs and paperwork.
4. *The senior has obligations, such as living in the house and maintaining it.* Also, "The requirement that the mortgage be paid back when the senior moves out of the house can be a real impediment if the senior wishes to move to a managed care facility. Typically, the proceeds of the house sale fund the entrance fee to the managed care facility. If the proceeds are instead used to pay off the

reverse mortgage, there may be nothing left to pay for managed care. Thus, a reverse mortgage only makes sense if the senior is absolutely certain she will not sell the house before death."

Her conclusion: "A reverse mortgage is the right solution for only a small minority of seniors. Only consider it if there are no other funds available and if the senior is certain she will remain in the home until death. Otherwise, selling the house and moving into a senior living facility usually makes a lot more sense."

A New York City CFP, David Finch, told me: "They are a last resort. They are evidence that your retirement planning failed. When I advise my young clients, I want them to wind up not needing a reverse mortgage."

While these are intelligent arguments, they overlook how eager many older people are to remain in their familiar houses in their familiar neighborhoods and how hostile many of them are to the idea of moving to a senior living facility. And they overlook the fact that many older people have too much house but not enough cash—and they are not necessarily destitute. They don't have needs; they have wants.

More arguments against reverse mortgages:

A lawyer, Joseph L. Matthews, has made these complaints about reverse mortgages in a popular book, *Long-Term Care: How to Plan & Pay for It* (5th edition, Nolo, 2004):

Complaint: Interest you owe is compounded: You pay interest on interest. Add to that the fact that, with a line of credit, the amount that you can borrow generally goes up. "The combination of these spiraling debt factors means that over a period of years, a modest initial reverse mortgage can cost considerably more than conventional forms of borrowing and can eat up all the equity in the property. An elder who wants to preserve some equity to pass on to heirs or to use in some other way after selling the house may instead wind up with a piece of property that has no residual value."

Comments: Paying interest on interest seems fair. The interest that someone owes, and postpones paying, is also a loan. And some people would rather that the interest accumulate with a reverse mortgage than have to pay their debts back quickly, as with a home-equity loan. Besides, the fact that your credit line increases (with a HECM) is considered a benefit of a reverse mortgage: You can get access to more money should you need it.

Sarah Hulbert of Seattle Mortgage emphasizes the fact that there are no payments required on a reverse mortgage until the loan becomes due.

Complaint: Another complaint that Matthews lodges: "A reverse mortgage also ties the borrower to the house. Most reverse mortgages require that the loan be repaid when the borrower no longer lives in the house. If the borrower moves in with relatives, moves to another area, or enters a nursing home to receive better care, monthly payments and any line of credit stop—and the borrower must repay the loan within a certain time. Elders who borrow under reverse mortgages may one day find themselves faced with the unhappy choice of paying off the loan in order to move to a more comfortable, healthy, or secure setting, or staying put to continue receiving the mortgage benefits."

Comments: So long as the borrower remains in the home for several years, the closing costs will not seem onerous. Also, presumably the homeowner considered the house he or she is living in to be comfortable, safe, and secure, or else the homeowner would have moved elsewhere instead of obtaining a reverse mortgage. In any case, having to remain in your old homestead for more than six months of the year in order to receive monthly payments—which will never end so long as you live in the house, even if your debt has long ago surpassed the value of the house—does not seem like cruel and unusual punishment.

Sarah Hulbert adds: "The majority of our borrowers seek out a reverse mortgage as a means to enable them to remain in the home (per AARP, 89 percent of seniors list the ability to remain in their home as their top priority when planning for retirement). While it does tie them to the home in some sense, it does so no more than a 'forward' mortgage would. The benefit is that the additional funds help them postpone (or eliminate altogether) the need to move."

On the other hand, no one promised you a rose garden. Reverse mortgages are not without fault. (See Exhibit 3.2.)

The closing costs, everyone admits, are quite high. But there are defenses.

Exhibit 3.2 The 12 Worst Things about Reverse Mortgages

1. They can be complicated and confusing.
2. If the homeowner leaves the house, or dies, soon after obtaining the mortgage, the cost of the loan will have been very high.
3. The homeowner's heirs will probably wind up with less of an inheritance.
4. Cash payments from a reverse mortgage are usually lower than the payments you might receive if you sold your house and invested the money in an income or immediate annuity.
5. Three days after signing a contract, you no longer can change your mind.
6. Homeowners receiving so much money to spend any way they wish may go haywire—and some have.
7. For a variety of reasons, seniors are the favorite targets of crooks and scam artists, and those with ready money from reverse mortgages may be especially vulnerable.
8. A senior may have better alternatives than a reverse mortgage, such as selling the house to a family member and then leasing it back, or selling the house to the family member in return for an annuity. Or selling the house and moving to a smaller one.
9. Unless the seniors are careful not to have much money in their accounts at the end of the month, the payments they receive might disqualify them for Social Security or Medicaid.
10. The closing costs are high.
11. If you have an unusually valuable house, you cannot get a HECM or Home Keeper reverse mortgage reflecting the house's true value. Your borrowing capacity is limited because reverse mortgages are targeted at the less well-to-do.
12. The interest rate is adjustable, so your debt could climb if rates in general go up.

Says Sarah Hulbert, "I never tell anyone this is cheap. But the closing costs can be covered by the loan, and fully financed. And if someone is going to live in a house for only a short time, we advise against a reverse mortgage. We're not salespeople. We're educators. If anyone needs extra money for only a short period of time, we tell them that a reverse mortgage is an expensive way to go."

Says Joseph DeMarkey of Bank of New York: "The main reason reverse mortgages are expensive is mortgage insurance, which can be as much as 2 percent of a property's value. On a $200,000 home, the closing costs could be $9,000 or 10,000, and $4,000 of that is mortgage insurance."

That mortgage insurance, he emphasizes, is necessary. Lenders don't have any idea when they will be repaid or what the home will eventually be worth or what will happen to interest rates. "If the homeowner lives to 120," he goes on, "if interest rates don't behave, and if real estate doesn't appreciate at 8 or 9 or 10 percent a year, the homeowner could wind up owing us money." But thanks to mortgage insurance, the lender won't wind up behind the eight ball.

Says DeMarkey firmly, "We wouldn't do reverse mortgages without that insurance. Because if the homeowner owes us $500,000 and the house is worth only $400,000, we can't sue the homeowner or attach other assets or go after the kids. That's why a reverse mortgage is more expensive."

Jeff Taylor of Wells Fargo is frustrated by all the talk about how expensive reverse mortgages are. "Compared to what?" he asks. "The cost of reverse mortgages is a particularly sensitive subject to me. This is not like other mortgages. You can live in your house the rest of your life, get a regular income, not pay anything back, and not even pay taxes on it. You don't have that guarantee with any other mortgage. Apart from the mortgage insurance, the closing costs are no different from any other mortgage." His company has published a short, incisive answer to some of the mythology circulated about reverse mortgages. (See Exhibit 3.3.)

Another objection is that reverse mortgages offer only adjustable interest rates, not fixed. And some older people insist on only fixed-rate mortgages. With a fixed-rate mortgage, if interest rates climb, borrowers need not pay more. "Even their kids don't want them to have an adjustable-rate mortgage," says one consultant with Wells Fargo.

Exhibit 3.3 The Four NEVERS

NEVER be forced to make a payment on the principal or interest until you move, sell the home, or die.

NEVER give up title to the house while you live there.

NEVER owe more than the sales price of the home.

NEVER be forced to move.

—Wells Fargo

But while an adjustable rate helps protect lenders in case rates spike up, there are limits on how high the rate on a reverse mortgage can go, thus protecting the borrower to a certain extent.

Undeniably, too, some borrowers have had disastrous results with reverse mortgages.

A report cited an article in the *Detroit Free Press* warns that reverse mortgages can become an expensive trap. It describes the experience of a couple that wasn't prepared for the large up-front fees that are higher than those for a conventional loan, years of high interest charges applied against their home, and the fact the spendable income received from a reverse mortgage is less than the home equity eaten up by the reverse mortgage.

Well, of course, a loan isn't free. The loan plus the interest you will owe is always going to be more than the money you wind up getting.

Besides, as mentioned, the up-front fees for a reverse mortgage are higher for a good reason: They include insurance, guarding the homeowner from being responsible should the value of the house not cover the amount of the loan.

The couple described in this newspaper article apparently spent too much. And if people take out a loan and proceed to squander the money, or spend it too quickly, that doesn't mean that there was something wrong with the terms of the loan.

Finally, if shady operators have managed to abuse reverse mortgages, it should come as no surprise. And they have. Do you remember when President Johnson was thinking of getting a heart transplant? He stipulated that the donor heart had to come from a banker. Why? He wanted a heart that had never been used.

In a legal case called "Elderly Reverse Mortgagors v TransAmerica Homefirst Corporation," a court in 2003 ordered TransAmerica and Metropolitan Life to pay $8 million to "lifetime" reverse-mortgage holders. The defendants were charged with "abusing elderly people in California by fraudulently concealing high costs and misrepresenting excessive charges in order to induce buyers to procure reverse mortgages.

"TranAmerica's strategy in this particular scheme was to use the high complexity of reverse mortgages to conceal certain excessive costs and fees that added tens of thousands of dollars to the cost of a reverse mortgage unnecessarily. In addition to these costs, six to ten years after a loan was issued, the mortgagor was required to purchase an annuity through MetLife as an integral part of the loan. The high cost of this annuity was charged to the buyer up front, and compound interest was charged on the cost, even though the mortgagor might never see any payments because of his or her age. The fact that compound interest was charged, and that there was no death benefit in the annuity, was concealed from the buyer.

"Because of these actions on the part of the defendants, many people found that they owed a great deal more at the end of their reverse mortgage than they had been led to believe. In the case of family members of elders who had purchased Homefirst reverse mortgages, many were surprised to find that when the senior passed away, the estate owed tens of thousands of dollars to Homefirst."

Finally, one of the biggest objections to a reverse mortgage is that you may have other, better alternatives, a subject we cover in a later chapter.

4

How Much Do You Really Know?

I love quizzes. Giving them, not taking them. This chapter consists of a quiz and is intended to test your knowledge of reverse mortgages and at the same time inform you of some curious and perhaps important rules.

1. *When a reverse-mortgage loan comes due, how long do you have to pay it off?*
   1. A month.
   2. Six months.
   3. A year.

Answer: C. A year, but if you submit a letter of intent, explaining any delay (for example, the heirs are fighting in court), you may be given an extension. HUD generally provides a six-month extension and may grant another six months.

2. *True or false? The first reverse mortgage saw the light of day in 1987.*

Answer: False. In 1961, Nelson Haynes of Deering Savings and Loan in Portland, Maine, issued the country's first reverse mortgage to Nellie Young, the widow of his high school football coach. The program was given a powerful boost in 1987, when the Department of Housing and Urban Development created its home equity conversion mortgage (HECM), providing insurance so that no borrowers would ever have to pay a lender more than their houses sold for.

3. *True or false? After you sign the papers to take out a reverse mortgage, you cannot change your mind.*

Answer: False. You have a three-day rescission period to change your mind.

4. *How many people may obtain a reverse mortgage together?*
   A. Two.
   B. Three.
   C. Four or more.

Answer: B. Three.

5. *True or false? If you change your mind after signing a contract, you may notify the lender in person or by phone.*

Answer: False. You must notify the lender in writing—by letter or fax.

6. *Yes or no? Because of physical or mental illness, you have not lived in your home for 12 consecutive months. Does this mean that your reverse-mortgage loan is due?*

Answer: Yes.

7. *Which of these properties is not eligible for a reverse mortgage?*
   A. Condominium.
   B. Cooperative.
   C. Second home.

Answer: A. Neither a cooperative nor a second home is eligible. (But a cooperative in New York state may be.)

8. *True or false? If you are in a chapter 13 bankruptcy, you may still get a reverse mortgage.*

Answer: True, but only if you get written permission from a judge. If you declare bankruptcy while you have a reverse mortgage, your loan may come due.

9. *True or false? You can change the way you receive your funds— monthly income, line of credit, lump sum—at any time.*

Answer: True, but there may be a $50 fee for such changes.

10. *Yes or no? One of the two borrowers moves out of the house. May the lender require repayment of the reverse mortgage?*

Answer: No, not until the second borrower moves out.

11. *Which of the following might make your loan come due immediately?*
    A. You rent out your house.
    B. You add a new owner.
    C. You buy a second house for cash.

Answer: A and B.

12. *True or false? Once you have decided whether you will get a monthly or yearly adjustable interest rate with a HECM mortgage, you cannot change your decision.*

Answer: True.

13. *A lender will normally estimate that a borrower will live how long?*
    A. To the particular person's life expectancy.
    B. To 90.
    C. To 100.

Answer: C.

14. *True or false? Unused funds in a Fannie Mae Home Keeper line of credit or Financial Freedom Cash Account do not grow, unlike the funds in a HECM.*

Answer: False.

15. *Which reverse mortgage forbids borrowers to make any repayments for five years?*
    A. Home Keeper.
    B. HECM.
    C. Financial Freedom.

Answer: C. The Financial Freedom Zero Point mortgage and Zero Cash account.

16. *What does LIBOR stand for?*

Answer: London interbank offered rate, used for determining the rates on some adjustable mortgages.

17. *What percentage of homes examined for reverse mortgages require repairs?*
    A. 20 percent.
    B. 50 percent.
    C. 86.7 percent.

Answer: B. Around 50 percent.

18. *Even if a spouse is not included in a reverse mortgage, because the spouse is under 62, both husband and wife must sign the deed at closing—if you live in a "homestead state." Do you live in one?*

Answer: These are homestead states: Alabama, Arizona, Arkansas, California, Colorado, Florida, Idaho, Illinois, Kansas, Kentucky, Minnesota, Missouri, Montana, New Hampshire, New Jersey, New Mexico, North Carolina, North Dakota, South Dakota, Tennessee, Texas, Vermont, Washington, West Virginia, Wisconsin, Wyoming, and the District of Columbia.

19. *True or false? If the sale of a house does not cover the amount of the loan, the contents of your home—furniture, jewelry, and so forth—can be used to satisfy the loan.*

Answer: False. (And who could think such a thing!)

20. *True or false? All reverse mortgages require a credit report.*

Answer: False. The Home Keeper does not.

21. *In what kind of dwelling do you not need a termite report to obtain a reverse mortgage?*
    A. Four-unit house.
    B. A kind of condominium.
    C. A houseboat.

Answer: B. A condominium above the first floor.

22. What percentage of seniors want to remain in their homes?
    A. 50 percent.
    B. 70 percent.
    C. 80 percent.

Answer: C. More than 80 percent, according to a poll by AARP.

23. *Your loan becomes due when you reach what age?*
    A. 100.
    B. 90.
    C. 150.

Answer: C. 150. Honest.

24 *Yes or no? If you use up all your credit or lump sum, can you obtain more money?*

Answer: Yes. You can refinance the loan if your house has appreciated. The closing costs will not be as high as they were when you first obtained the mortgage.

25. *True or false? The typical borrower is unmarried, 76, and female, and the typical loan amount is $170,000.*

Answer: True.

26. *Yes or no? Is a reverse-mortgage borrower always required to pay off existing mortgage debt?*

Answer: Not always. The lender of the earlier mortgage may agree to subordinate the loan to the reverse mortgage. Usually only state or local government lenders will do this. But generally lenders don't want their loans to be subordinate to other debt.

27. *Yes or no? If a 62-year-old with a 52-year-old spouse takes the younger spouse off the title so as to qualify for a reverse mortgage, can the older spouse put the younger spouse back on the title when that spouse reaches the age of 62 without triggering repayment of the loan?*

Answer: Yes, but the terms must be renegotiated because the ages of the borrowers and their expected longevity have changed.

28. *Yes or no? When a borrower sells a house to pay off a reverse mortgage, are broker's commissions and other expenses subtracted to produce the selling price?*

Answer: Yes.

5

Consider the Interesting Alternatives

The ideal candidates for a reverse mortgage (1) need money, (2) will continue to need money, (3) are eager to remain in their house, and (4) own a valuable house without a sizable mortgage. But a reverse mortgage isn't free. Besides the high closing costs, the loan plus interest must be paid back, sooner or later, thus reducing your wealth and shrinking or even eliminating any inheritance you might have planned to bestow upon your heirs. And in case you still believe that reverse mortgages are gifts from above, be advised that another name for them is "rising debt, falling equity loans."

Getting a reverse mortgage is like invading principal, something that many people are averse to doing—especially the wealthy. Still, invading principal is a sensible thing to do when you need money or if your investment portfolio is not well diversified.

In any case, there are reasonable alternatives to reverse mortgages. There are things you can do instead—and things you might do along with getting a reverse mortgage.

Here are seven possibilities that seniors and people advising them should consider:

1. Sell the house to the children.
2. Investigate public programs for the needy.
3. Get a home-equity loan or a line of credit.
4. Buy an income annuity.
5. Move to a less expensive area and into a less expensive house.
6. Economize.
7. Get a job, or a new job.

1. Sell the house to the children. One of the best alternatives is that your children buy your house from you and then rent it back to you for as long as you want to live there, perhaps in exchange for an annuity, a lifetime stream of payments, that they provide. Or in exchange for the house, they simply buy you an annuity from a private company.

The parents have thus eliminated the high closing costs of a reverse mortgage, yet the parents remain in the house. And if they decide to leave—because of illness, perhaps—they will not have blown a lot of money on those closing costs.

Also, the children continue to own the family homestead, which very likely will be worth more in the future. There should be no disappointment about the parents' spending down the children's possible inheritance, as might happen with a reverse mortgage.

Any income the parents receive from their children should be tax-free, unless their capital gains are especially high. As for the children, they obtain the tax advantages of owning rental real estate.

Possible problems: The children may not have the money to swing the deal. Or they may disagree among themselves about how to arrange matters ("They sent you through medical school, so I deserve the house," or "You have only one child, and I have four."). Afterward, like King Lear's kids (apart from Cordelia), they may not fulfill their promises to support their parents. Also, they must pay full price for the house or the IRS might conclude that they have made a gift and owe gift taxes.

Mike Gruley of First Financial Mortgage mentions Polonius's advice in *Hamlet*: "Neither a borrower nor a lender be." Latent competition between family members may be revived. Or a child's spouse may become ill and suddenly stop the payments. One counselor reports, "I've seen the children promise $1,000 a month, but soon it became too big a toll."

Clearly, the parents and their children must consult a lawyer, perhaps an elder-care lawyer (see Chapter 7) so that there is paperwork to indicate what everyone's obligations are.

Few children actually buy their parents' houses, but I know of a family in which the parents simply exchanged houses with their children, who were living on the same street. The parents' house was too large, the children's house was too small (what with their own children), and the older couple wanted to move down, the younger couple to move up. Moving was a cinch. The day of the big move, all the neighbors came to watch.

Stacey Stuber, a counselor with Momentive Credit Counseling in Indiana, has been advising people about reverse mortgages for eight years, and only once has she seen a parent-children transaction. A woman's five children bought her home and then leased it back to her. "They had the money, and they didn't want her to pay the closing costs on a reverse mortgage."

2. Investigate public programs for the needy. If your finances (or those of your parents) are in sorry shape, you (or they) may be entitled to public assistance. There are a good many local, state, and federal programs for the needy, even though they may not be well publicized.

Get in touch with your area's agency on aging—AAA. Call 800-677-1116. This agency may help you with everything from reduced property taxes to lowering the cost of prescription drugs.

Also get in touch with www.BenefitsCheckup.org, a source of information sponsored by the National Council on Aging. You fill out a questionnaire, without giving your name. You may also contact BenefitsCheckup.org, which can find programs suitable for you; it also tells you how to apply for them.

People over age 65 may be eligible for monthly payments from Supplemental Security Income, SSI. In 2005, to qualify for SSI your cash and savings must have totaled less than $2,000–$3,000 for a couple.

Usually certain assets do not count, such as a home, one car, and a small savings account for burial expenses. Your unearned income (from stocks and bonds, for example, not from a job) cannot be more than $599—or $899 for a couple.

If you work and therefore have earned income, the income limits are higher. The income limits are also higher in states that add something to your SSI. And if you can receive SSI, you may also qualify for other public benefits. You can obtain information from AARP at 800-772-1213.

You can receive public benefits and still obtain a reverse mortgage. In fact, you will have less need for cash advances, and, because you get less money, your interest charges will be less. But beware of losing your public benefits by getting too much income from a reverse mortgage. Cash from a loan that remains in a savings or checking account at the end of a calendar month is counted as an asset by SSI and other programs. So you can be dropped from the program. Lesson: limit your loans to what you can spend in a month.

For information on SSI, go to www.ssa.gov/ssi. Or phone 800-772-1213.

There are also deferred payment loans (DPLs) available for repairing your house. State and local governments may offer them, and usually they are limited to homeowners with moderate incomes. No repayment is required as long as the homeowners live in their house. DPLs cost very little, but they may be hard to find. For help, phone local agencies that help older people.

In addition, property-tax deferral loans (PTDs) are offered by some state and local government agencies. This type of reverse mortgage provides loans that can be used to pay property taxes. No repayment is needed while someone lives in his or her home. Usually they are for people age 65 and over who have moderate incomes. Phone your local property-tax commissioner.

The following states may offer PTDs, as reported by AARP: Arizona, California, Colorado, Florida, Georgia, Illinois, Iowa, Maine, Maryland, Massachusetts, Michigan, Minnesota, New Hampshire, North Dakota, Oregon, Pennsylvania, South Dakota, Tennessee, Texas, Utah, Virginia, Washington, Wisconsin, Wyoming, and the District of Columbia.

Connecticut (860-571-3502) and Montana (406-841-2840) offer special reverse-mortgage loans; the Connecticut plan is limited to the severely disabled.

3. Get a home-equity loan or a line of credit. These are second mortgages, and the interest you pay on them is tax-deductible (up to $100,000, or not more than your house is worth).

A home-equity loan (HEL) gives you a lump sum, and the interest rate is fixed. Best use: one-time expenses, like remodeling a house.

A home-equity line of credit (HELOC) gives you an open line of credit, with a specific limit. The interest rate is changed monthly, not yearly, as with most adjustable-rate loans, and the caps are higher. Recently the rates were lower than those on home-equity loans. But those rates can quickly leap skyward. Best use: as an emergency fund, or for ongoing costs. These are recommended for loans that may take more than three years to repay.

One elder-care lawyer insists that he knows of a loan even better than a reverse mortgage. You get a home-equity line of credit instead. Usually it has no closing costs at all, unlike the steep charges of a reverse mortgage. In addition the interest rate may be the same as with a reverse mortgage. And every month, you just withdraw what you need for as long as you want to live in your home. This is an interesting idea that may be a bit flawed: See what Joseph M. DeMarkey of the Bank of New York Mortgage has to say on the subject:

I love HELOCs. I have one myself, and HELOCs are often compared to reverses. In fact, it is our experience that when prospects do not take out an RM [reverse mortgage], they take out a HELOC—unless they sell the home.

HELOCs are not "better" than RMs or vice versa. They are different in several ways:

(a) Lenders will look at a borrower's income and credit when making a decision on a HELOC—unlike an RM, which does not have any credit/income criteria. Often seniors will not qualify for the amount of capital they want to borrow due to their low incomes.

(b) Borrowers must make regular payments on HELOCs (not on an RM) and

(c) HELOCs have a finite life (10 years, for example), then the loan must be paid in full at the maturity date. (RMs have no maturity date.)

So while at first blush that attorney might be on the right track, I think his theory gets derailed when you look at the specific situation of many senior homeowners.

Besides, the longer you live in a house with a home-equity loan, the more likely you are to run out of money. That's not true of a reverse mortgage.

Sarah Hulbert of Seattle Mortgage recalls a borrower who obtained a home-equity loan and two years later could no longer make the payments. It was a vicious circle, her trying to use the loan to pay back her debt. She then obtained a reverse mortgage, which she used to pay off her home-equity loan—and that worked out satisfactorily.

"It boils down to suitability," Hulbert continues. "Which product best meets your needs. If you need cash short term, a home-equity loan may be best. If you need long-term cash flow, a reverse mortgage may be best."

Mike Gruley mentions another formidable drawback of HELs: "You can be forced out of your home if you don't make regular payments."

In short, a reverse mortgage is easier to get, and easier to live with, than a home-equity loan. And, as Jeff Taylor of Wells Fargo points out, with a reverse mortgage you get a government guarantee that you will continue to be paid, and assurance that you will never owe more than the amount your house could sell for.

Some other things wrong with home-equity loans, as ticked off by *Money Magazine* (September 2005):

- If you get an interest-only loan, the minimum payments will be relatively small. But, after 10 years, when the loan matures, you must begin repaying principal—and your monthly payments would leap up. (*Solution:* when you obtain the mortgage, sign up for a fully amortized loan program, in which you pay back principal along with interest.)
- Because it's an adjustable-rate loan, the rate can rise fairly quickly. And painfully. (*Solution:* if you think you need more than three years to pay off your HELOC, get a home-equity loan instead. In three years, a low initial rate can climb sky-high.)
- You may be hit with new fees. Today most lenders have early-termination fees on their HELOCS—if the line of credit is closed within three years. The cost is typically a few hundred dollars, but some lenders charge a percentage of the balance or even insist on receiving transaction costs that were supposedly waived earlier. And

now there are even inactivity fees ($50) if people don't use their lines of credit for (typically) a year. There may also be a yearly fee of $50.

- Some people go a little loony with sudden access to a big pot of money—lottery winner syndrome. One survey found that 13 percent of HELOC borrowers used the money for travel or other leisure activities. The old admonition is, Don't lose your house for a blouse. (With a reverse mortgage, borrowers may go bonkers, too, but not, perhaps, when they receive a monthly income.)
- Many authorities urge people to consolidate their debts into one home-equity loan. The interest rate will not only be lower than with a credit card or personal loan, but the interest will be tax-deductible (up to $100,000). Trouble is, you are substituting an unsecured loan for a secured loan. A credit-card company cannot attach your house; a bank that gave you a home-equity mortgage can.

4. Buy an income annuity. You could sell the house, or get a home-equity loan, and with the proceeds buy an income annuity. A good many financial planners recommend this to their clients.

An income annuity has some advantages over even a reverse mortgage. It doesn't ever stop while you are alive, unlike the monthly income from a reverse mortgage, which ends when you leave your house. Also, there are income annuities (called variable annuities) that may be invested in stocks, giving you a possible defense against inflation. And an income annuity generally pays more than the payments received from a reverse mortgage.

But the case for a reverse mortgage is stronger simply because the payments are not taxable, and some of the annuity payments may be.

Robert Nestor, a principal with the Vanguard Group, explains: with an income annuity purchased with after-tax money, a piece of each payment is a return of your cost basis and not taxable. (It's roughly equal to your cost basis divided by your expected mortality, based on IRS tables.) With an annuity purchased with pretax dollars, all would be taxable.

If seniors do decide on an income annuity, they must answer a couple of questions:

- Should they use all their cash to buy such an annuity, so they receive a nice, fat regular income for as long as they live?

- Should they buy an income annuity that will pay their survivors for ten years after they themselves are gone? So, if they don't die soon after getting the annuity, they don't lose all that money?

The answer that Vanguard's Nestor gives to both these questions is: probably not.

Don't put everything you own into an income annuity because you may need money for emergencies. Maybe, he suggests, buy such an annuity with no more than 50 percent of your assets.

Buying a "10 years certain" policy—which many people do—is expensive and undermines the whole idea behind such annuities, in that an insurance company balances people who die relatively early (and forfeit some money) against people who live almost as long as Methusaleh and really clean up.

There's more interest in income annuities these days, reports Nestor, because of worries people have about the solidity of Social Security and corporate pension plans. After all, the only surefire way to never run out of money—apart from printing your own—is to own an income annuity.

Which wording does Nestor prefer? "Immediate" annuity? Or "income" or "payout" annuity? He prefers "income" because it's descriptive. The word he is a little unhappy with is "annuity" because it comes with rather nasty baggage.

An income annuity's opposite is a "deferred" annuity, an investment in which you are supposed to withdraw your money sometime in the distant future. It's thanks to deferred annuities that the reputation of all annuities has been tarred—because of the way they have been sold, as a scheme to avoid taxes. Many deferred annuities are also expensive and come with painful early-withdrawal penalties, which can last for 10 or more years. Many people now selling deferred annuities, I suspect, once sold tax-sheltered limited partnerships, and, before that, snake oil.

By way of explanation, deferred annuities can be either "fixed" (the money has been invested in a long-term bond) or "variable" (it has been invested in securities whose value may change, like stocks).

Someone with a deferred variable annuity, even with its tax-postponed status, would have to hold on for at least 10 years to wind up ahead of a stock mutual fund. To come out ahead of an index fund, which is all but immune to taxes anyway, someone would have to hold on for 30 or 40 years.

Deferred annuities also have some negative tax aspects:

- Money that comes out of a deferred annuity is taxed at your highest tax bracket. "You give up favorable capital-gains treatment," says Nestor.
- As mentioned, if you annuitize an annuity (take regular with-drawals), some of the money that comes out is considered taxable income. (This is true only if you bought the annuity after 1986.)
- If someone dies holding an annuity, his or her heirs inherit the annuity at the original owner's tax basis. In other words, they pay taxes on the dead person's capital gains.
- Tax deferment is not that big a deal anymore, what with long-term capital gains being taxed at only a maximum of 15 percent.

In short, don't confuse variable deferred annuities with income annuities. (Not that those other annuities don't have a place, providing they aren't expensive, don't have premature withdrawal penalties, and are appropriate for a particular person.)

In 2004, sad to report, some 22 percent of all people buying variable annuities were over age 60, and they faced stiff penalties if they took their money out in fewer than six years. Meanwhile, brokers and finan-cial advisers who sold these annuities could come away with commis-sions as lofty as 10 percent.

Why should someone buy an income annuity rather than an income mutual fund, such as Vanguard LifeStrategy Income? (An income fund combines bonds with high-yielding stocks.)

"At the end of the day," Nestor answered, "the LifeStrategy Fund will probably be better for you." It has lower administrative costs, investors have more control over it, and they can leave it to their heirs.

But even with such a fund, you may run out of money. You may spend more than 4 percent (the magic number) of your assets every year, and that may leave you destitute in your old, old age. If you take out 5 or 7 percent, he pointed out, there's a not negligible chance that you'll wind up broke. Besides which, when people know that they can't run out of money, they tend to spend more and worry less. Maybe people should consider getting both—if they can.

There are problems with an income annuity, too, Nestor pointed out. There's a lack of liquidity: no ready cash. And a person could lose the "bet." The day after someone buys an immediate annuity, that person might buy the farm. All that money gone! (Actually, as Nestor notes, it's a sensible bet. All insurance, in fact, is a bet. If you buy life insurance and live a long time before your heirs collect, you have "lost" the bet. The same goes for buying auto insurance and never having an accident.)

Another drawback of an income annuity is that the interest rate doesn't change. and inflation can make that interest rate look fairly stingy, especially if you live from, say, ages 70 to 90.

"We strongly recommend that people stagger their annuities," Nestor said. Buy annuities at different times, with different interest rates. Rates seem low now, he noted, although some people argue that they may stay where they are or go even lower.

Should a husband and wife buy an income annuity together? "It makes sense," he said. With a couple, one of them could live to age 90 or even to age 100.

What about variable-income annuities, those that invest in stocks? It seems sensible to have around 20 percent of an income in the stock market, I said. "We think so, too," he replied, and Vanguard offers a whole slew of variable-income annuities, modeled on some of its more well-known mutual funds, as well as an equity-index income annuity, which invests a varying percentage of its assets in the Standard & Poor's 500 stock index.

But variable annuities have captured a very small percentage of the marketplace. "People don't understand it," he said. "It's counter-intuitive. They want a guaranteed income, and here their payments may fluctuate."

A devastating critique of variable-income annuities, linked to an index of the stock market, has come from Larry Swedroe, a money manager who is a passionate advocate of index funds. They could be "poster boys" for products that are too good to be true, he has written in a paper circulated on the Internet, "They are also good examples of why investors should avoid products that are complex." This complexity, he goes on, almost always winds up favoring the seller and not the buyer. (He was not writing about Vanguard's products.)

The minimum Vanguard accepts for an income annuity is $20,000. The oldest age someone can apply for one is 85. There's no minimum age, but Nestor discourages young people from getting them—the older you are, the better they pay.

What's a good age to buy one? After you retire, perhaps in your late 60s or early 70s, and if you could use a regular source of income. But if, as it is, you're spending only 2 or 3 percent of your assets each year, said Nestor, you probably don't need one.

Warning: Advances from an annuity reduce SSI benefits dollar for dollar and can make you ineligible for Medicaid.

The four basic types of annuities are tax deferred with variable investment return, tax deferred with fixed investment return, immediate income with variable investment return, and immediate income with fixed investment return. These are summarized in Exhibit 5.1.

5. Move to a less expensive area and into a less expensive house. This has been called "geographical arbitrage"—moving to another area when you retire, a place where expenses are much lower. Or moving to another place while you're still working, but where the pay is much higher. Or moving abroad. (See Exhibit 5.2 for the tax angles.)

Exhibit 5.1 Four types of annuities.

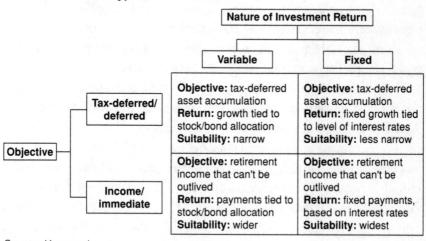

		Nature of Investment Return	
		Variable	**Fixed**
Objective	**Tax-deferred/ deferred**	**Objective:** tax-deferred asset accumulation **Return:** growth tied to stock/bond allocation **Suitability:** narrow	**Objective:** tax-deferred asset accumulation **Return:** fixed growth tied to level of interest rates **Suitability:** less narrow
	Income/ immediate	**Objective:** retirement income that can't be outlived **Return:** payments tied to stock/bond allocation **Suitability:** wider	**Objective:** retirement income that can't be outlived **Return:** fixed payments, based on interest rates **Suitability:** widest

Source: Vanguard.

Exhibit 5.2 Taxes on Selling Your Home

If you are considering moving instead of getting a reverse mortgage or another alternative, familiarize yourself with the tax rules.

- You can exclude from taxes up to $500,000 of the capital gains tax from the sale of your home if you are married and file a joint return. Singles can exclude up to $250,000.
- The residence can be a condominium, a manufactured or modular home, a recreational vehicle, or a houseboat.
- You must not have used the exclusion within the past two years.
- You must have owned the home for at least two years.
- You must have used it as your principal residence for two of the five years before the sale.

If you don't meet these requirements because of, for example, illness, you are entitled to a proportional exclusion amount based on how long you actually lived in the house.

Source: IRS.

The trouble with these tactics, as Fred Brock points out in his book *Live Well on Less Than You Think,* is that a place where expenses are low probably has mostly low-paying jobs or few jobs. And a place where the salaries are high is probably a place where expenses are high, too.

Brock, who sold his house in Montclair, New Jersey, to take a job in Kansas, has a solution to the problem of geographical arbitrage: look for places where the costs are low and where job growth looks good.

As for the state and local taxes as a percentage of income, New York is highest at 12.9 percent. Lowest is Alaska at 6.3 percent. New Jersey is 15th at 10.1 percent. Sixth from the bottom is Florida, at 8.8 percent. To check out the cost of living in various communities, go to www.BestPlaces.net. To check taxes, go to www.RetirementLiving.com.

College towns are usually a good bet because of their low crime rate, low cost of living, and high state of culture, plus good hospitals. And if money is not really a hindrance, take the test at www.BestPlaces.net to discover what your dream locale really is. (The site seems to favor Boston.) This site also lets you compare expenses in the place you're living in now with the place you're interested in moving to—in housing, food and groceries, transportation, utilities, health care, sales taxes, auto insurance, and so on.

Consumer Reports Money Adviser looked at three best-selling retirement planning guides to see which locales, if any, all the authors agreed on. Only five spots managed to make all three lists: Asheville, North Carolina; Fort Collins, Colorado; Medford-Ashland, Oregon; Sarasota, Florida; and Tucson, Arizona.

What kinds of people can just up and move to a new place, especially when they are somewhat long in the tooth? Are we talking about outgoing people who make new friends easily? Along with people who are introverted and don't need new friends, who just need books and libraries and concert halls and walking trails?

Selling your house and moving to a smaller place nearby may be a more reasonable solution. There is less change and less challenge. But you should check the math. How much cash will you free up? What will it cost to buy a new home and maintain it, or to rent a new place?

Don't think of trading down as necessarily exchanging your comfortable big house in the suburbs for a shack in Shantytown. You might buy a small condo on the beach or a high-rise apartment in the city—with doorpeople, swimming pool, and good restaurants nearby. Living in an apartment house, with maintenance people readily available, and no snow to shovel or grass to mow or gutters to clean, has something to recommend it.

Because you have been around the block a few times, you can make a sensible choice. As you know, there are sometimes true bargains available in housing—"creampuffs," for example, being sold by other seniors who cannot believe that their houses have appreciated as much as their agents claim. You can look for houses especially suitable for seniors, too, those on one floor, without huge yards that require maintenance, within walking distance of shopping.

Bear in mind that if you sell your home and move to a smaller place, your expenses may go down. You will have less house to heat and cool, less lawn to mow and care for, less roof to replace if it fails. Your property taxes may also go down. So will your home insurance. Besides, a smaller place is easier to clean. And, in moving, you can get rid of some of the furniture, clothing, and books that you have accumulated over the years. In fact, ridding your house of clutter can be a special joy. You may have to ask your local garbage-collection department to make a special trip after you have had your garage sales.

There are some downsides to moving. You will probably have a real estate commission to pay, which will likely be 6 or 7 percent of the price your receive for your home. (The cost of a reverse mortgage, meanwhile, may be only 4 or 5 percent of a home's value.) And you'll have closing costs to pay when you buy a new home. But if you use the same agent to sell and buy, you may be able to bargain down the commission. There will also be moving costs plus the hassle of canceling this and starting that—telephone service, insurance, mail delivery.

You might also use a discount broker and perhaps pay as little as a 2 percent commission. Check out www.Assist2sell.com. Then there's www.ZipRealty.com, which charges 5 percent but gives you 20 percent of the commission back.

To get a rough idea of what your house is worth, ask three real estate agents. Or go to zillow.com, which gives you an estimate based on recent sales and on tax rates.

Although trading down is a possible alternative to a reverse mortgage, your decision about whether to move or to get a reverse mortgage may depend upon how eager you are to remain in the house you are living in now and how much you want to avoid changes in your life.

If you want to buy another house and obtain a reverse mortgage at the same time, consider Fannie Mae's Home Keeper for Purchase Loan, described in Chapter 10.

In my own case, I sold my house for an obscene profit and rented an apartment in a building with doorpeople, a swimming pool, and supposedly a gym (it never materialized). But I have another house, a smaller one, in the country, and I visit it whenever I desperately miss mowing the lawn, cleaning the gutters, raking the leaves, and so forth.

Still, as Greg Daugherty writes in *Consumer Reports Money Adviser* (May 2005), renting has drawbacks. The rent may go up. Your lease may not be renewed, and out you must go. Besides, in most areas, not many single-family houses are for rent—just apartments.

On the other hand, landlords tend to favor retirees because they are typically less destructive and less noisy than younger tenants. So older people may get the most desirable rentals, and at good prices. To check which is better, renting or buying, go to www.ginniemae.gov and use its Buy Vs. Rent Calculator.

A more drastic move is to retire outside your home country. Truth is, though, that many people who move abroad wind up returning because they miss friends, relatives, and familiar surroundings. Indeed, people who move to a foreign area because of their jobs are apt to become depressed.

But Baby Boomers, 78 million of them, are supposedly more adventuresome, and may seek out places where the living is easier and the climate more hospitable.

No doubt the more successful and the less homesick will be those people who have lived abroad before or who are returning to their native countries.

Just as career-switchers are likely to be more successful if they make a 45-degree switch (nurse to physician) rather than a 90-degree switch (nurse to accountant), the more successful emigrants may move to countries where English is spoken, like Canada or Bermuda.

Even so, Mexico, Costa Rica, and Panama are reputed to be popular retirement areas, along with Nicaragua, Honduras, Ecuador, and English-speaking Belize, according to an article in *The New York Times* (July 30, 2005, p. C5).

Emigrants crow about the low cost of housing and help and the savings in utility bills and auto insurance. But they should also consider political instability, the quality of medical services, police corruption, and the strength of local financial institutions like banks.

Be sure to vacation in a foreign country before you decide to move there. Chat with people in the local expatriate community. The *Times* writer, Hillary Chura, suggests asking them about the size of the tarantulas.

Before moving abroad, ask yourself whether the exchange rate is favorable. What about the cost of traveling back and forth to the United States? How will you obtain health care? (Medicare is good only in the United States.) What taxes will you pay? Are foreigners allowed to buy property? A useful Web site for this information is www.internationalliving.com.

6. Economize. Brock argues, "With proper maintenance, keeping a car for ten years or more does not [necessarily] mean big repair problems because cars built nowadays are so much better than in the past."

You might also raise the deductibles on any insurance policies you own and get lower collision coverage on your car. You could eat out less often or at less expensive places; you could take advantage of "early bird" specials or visit salad bars. In addition you could rent movies rather than visit theaters and get an intermediary telephone service, like USA Datanet, which costs far less than regular providers. Also, you could drop your cell phone service after asking yourself whether you really need it.

Finally, subscribe to *Consumer Reports,* or read it regularly in a library. If you follow its advice, whatever you buy—a car, a washing machine, a digital camera—should last longer and require fewer repairs.

But don't go overboard. Don't give up your morning coffee if that morning coffee is all that's keeping you from coming down with a bad case of the blues. If I myself had followed the advice I once read about saving a few bucks by giving my own kid a haircut while he was growing up, he could not have appeared in public for months, and years later I would probably have had to pay a psychiatrist to explore the origins of the kid's Oedipal rage.

7. Get a job, or a new job. Jobs for older people generally do not pay well and are certainly not glamorous, but there's a firm link between someone's health and keeping busy.

AARP is working with several companies interested in hiring older people, including Home Depot. To learn more, go to www.aarp.org/ featuredemployers. Other helpful Web sites include www.retiredbrains.com, www.seniorjobbank.org, thephoenixlink.com (for executives), and www.yourencore.com (for experienced scientists).

Having a job may mean that some of your Social Security income will be taxed, depending on your age. See Exhibit 5.3.

Tip: When an interview is coming to an end, the last thing you might say (if it's true) is: "If you offer me this job, I'll take it." Interviewers like to know that they can save time and effort by offering a job to someone who won't turn it down. Your full retirement age (FRA), for Social Security purposes, is when you are entitled to full Social Security retirement benefits. If you were born in 1937 or earlier, your full retirement

Exhibit 5.3 Working and Social Security

Year of Birth	Full Retirement Age
1937 or earlier	65
1938	65 and 2 months
1939	65 and 4 months
1940	65 and 6 months
1941	65 and 8 months
1942	65 and 10 months
1943–1954	66
1955	66 and 2 months
1956	66 and 4 months
1957	66 and 6 months
1958	66 and 8 months

age is 65. If you choose to receive benefits earlier than your FRA, your payments will be lower. And if you continue working while collecting Social Security benefits before your FRA, your benefits may be reduced.

Lesson: If you want to continue working, try to wait until you reach FRA—which may be only a matter of months.

6

Are You the Perfect Customer?

Two different kinds of people are good candidates for a reverse mortgage.

1. People who *need* cash.
2. People who *want* more cash.

Let's start with people who are needy.

Stephen Pepe of Community Service Network in Stoneham, Massachusetts, a reverse-mortgage counselor, believes that the ideal borrower is someone "frustrated with his or her lack of income. It's preventing that person from leading a worry-free existence. Folks having a hard time making ends meet."

A good example is provided by Bill Agner of the Mortgage Network in Indianapolis, who tells of a couple in a happy marriage, living on a decent income from his pension and his Social Security—$4,000 a month. They didn't need extra money.

Then he died.

The money the wife had been receiving from the husband's Social Security and pension sank, and her income plummeted to between $700 and $800 a month.

She then obtained a reverse mortgage, paid off her existing mortgage, and chose a monthly income payout—$250 a month for the rest of her life. That meant that instead of her being $300 in debt every month, she cleared $800 to $900. "She's had to reduce her lifestyle some," says Agner, "but she's staying in her home."

Other typical borrowers include older people living on a fixed income who have trouble paying big bills, like property taxes or car repairs. Or they may include a widow who doesn't have the money or skill to repair her house, which is going downhill. (Widows, in fact, make up a large percentage of the people who obtain reverse mortgages.)

The second group of people suitable for reverse mortgages includes the fairly well-to-do. They do not have trouble making ends meet. But they are after something more. As Agner puts it, they want to improve their lifestyle. They want to travel, to dine out more, to buy new clothes, to make gifts to their children and grandchildren, to remodel their house. To live a little higher on the hog.

Many of them obtain the mortgages offered by Financial Freedom, which can provide giant loans (including one to a woman with an $18 million house).

Stacey Stuber of Momentive Credit Counseling recalls a client with an expensive home and $500,000 in stocks—stocks she did not want to sell. "That's not typical, but there is a certain percentage of borrowers who have other assets they want to keep."

What do these two groups of people—the "needers" and the "wanters"—have in common? An investment portfolio that is out of whack. They have a surplus of house and a paucity of cash. They might own a $200,000 house but no stocks or bonds worth talking about, or a $10 million house along with securities they don't want to sell. In both cases, their houses are occupying too large a place in their portfolios. And because they cannot sell a third bedroom or a downstairs bathroom to raise money, they will take out a loan against their house to boost their cash holdings and thus bring their portfolios closer to being in balance.

Are You the Perfect Customer?

No, every candidate for a reverse mortgage is not house rich and cash poor. But every reasonable candidate owns a lopsided portfolio in which the house constitutes the lop side.

Here's a checklist. Fill it out to see whether you may be an ideal client.

- ☐ You and your spouse are 62 years of age or older.
- ☐ The house in question is your principal residence.
- ☐ You live in the house at least six months of the year.
- ☐ For a HECM, your residence is a single-family house, a duplex, a triplex, a four-unit residence, or a condominium. Even a manufactured home may be eligible. However, it cannot be a cooperative, an apartment in which the tenants own everything in common (except in New York state). For a Fannie Mae Home Keeper mortgage, you must own a single-family home or a condominium.
- ☐ You have a lot of equity in your house—the value of the house minus whatever mortgage you still have outstanding. ("Equity" is your free-and-clear ownership of the house.)
- ☐ You do not plan to move out in a year or two. In a year or two, you are not going to decide that you prefer a warmer climate, a house with fewer stairs, or a house overlooking an enchanting body of water.
- ☐ You have a continual need for cash to pay your bills and to improve your way of life.
- ☐ You are not receiving Supplemental Security Income or money from other public programs that might be imperiled if you obtained a reverse mortgage. Even your eligibility for Medicaid, the government program for the needy (as opposed to Medicare), might be endangered if you obtained a reverse mortgage.
- ☐ Your spouse has no misgivings.
- ☐ You have consulted with your children. They are in favor of your getting such a mortgage and are happy to sit in on the planning sessions.

☐ You are not determined to leave your house, free and clear, to your children.

☐ You know that a reverse mortgage is not a 62nd-birthday present. It is a loan. And it is more expensive than most other mortgages because of the insurance and closing costs. Even AARP, a powerful advocate of reverse mortgages, in its booklet *Home-made Money* warns: "A reverse mortgage can be an expensive way to borrow money."

☐ You have considered the alternatives, such as a home-equity loan and buying a smaller, less expensive house.

☐ You don't own stocks and bonds that you could sell to improve your cash flow but that you are holding on to for not the best of reasons such as: You don't want to pay any capital-gains taxes; you think these securities will appreciate much more; you have losses and are determined to break even; you once worked for the company and want to remain loyal; or your beloved Aunt Tillie left you these securities, and they have a sentimental value.

☐ You have a good reason to hold on to your securities; they help diversify your portfolio. You know that even residential real estate can take a big hit (what if a major employer in your town moves out?) and that owning some stocks and some bonds can keep your portfolio afloat if the worst happens.

☐ You know what you will be using the money for, and the number of frivolous things you will purchase is small. You are not going to go haywire with the money and buy a LearJet or take a $75,000 trip around the world unless you are sure you can afford it.

☐ You know that the time you have to change your mind, after signing the papers, is just three days.

☐ If you have decided on a monthly income, you are reasonably sure that it will be sufficient. If you have decided on a lump sum, you are reasonably sure that that will solve most if not all of your financial problems. If you have decided on a line of credit, you are reasonably sure that it is more suitable than a monthly income or a lump sum.

- ☐ You have consulted a counselor, and that person has answered your questions.

- ☐ No one has urged you to obtain a reverse mortgage and then use the money to buy life insurance, a deferred annuity, or whatever else from that person.

7

Where to Get Good, Unbiased Advice

You can spend your reverse-mortgage on anything under the sun that you want to, with one glaring exception: You cannot use any money from the HUD-sponsored mortgage, the HECM, to pay someone for advising you about a reverse mortgage.

When reverse mortgages first came out, certain "estate planners" began giving people advice, sometimes charging them up to $10,000. The government sued to forbid this and won.

After all, you can get free advice about reverse mortgages from knowledgeable and sympathetic people: counselors. If you have other financial needs, by all means consult a financial planner or an elder-law attorney or an accountant. But for the real skinny on reverse mortgages, head for a counselor.

Reverse-Mortgage Counselors

The counselors I have interviewed have uniformly been warm and winning, probably because they were carefully selected and because they are in the enviable and rare position of having jobs that they enjoy and where they know that they are doing good. Many counselors tell me with genuine delight how pleased they are when old-timers tell them that their reverse mortgage was a lifesaver.

To obtain a HECM, the popular reverse mortgage sponsored by HUD, or a Fannie Mae Home Keeper, or the Cash Account from Financial Freedom, you are required to have a chat with a counselor who works for a nonprofit or public agency that has been approved by HUD. Usually it's free.

To find a HECM counselor in your area, go to www.hecmresources.org/network.cfm or call AARP at 800-209-8085, Monday to Friday from 7 a.m. to 12 midnight Eastern time. For a list of counseling agencies, go to www.hud.gov/offices/hsg/sfh/hecm/hecmlist.cfm. Ask whether an agency charges a fee.

Almost everyone agrees that the classiest counselors are the AARP-certified counselors, who are specially trained and specially selected. "They are the gold standard," says Linda Tyndal, a counselor with Pierce County Community Service in Washington state.

AARP counselors usually spend at least an hour with applicants, and there is no charge. Sessions are in person if local, by telephone if not local. (But these days, says Tyndal, counselors are so busy that you will be lucky to get even a phone appointment soon.) If the appointment is by phone, two or more sessions are typical. The counselors talk about the different types of reverse mortgages and the alternatives.

After a counseling session, the would-be borrower will receive a Certificate of HECM Counseling. It remains valid for 180 days, and the prospect must give it to the reverse-mortgage lender when he or she submits an application. It is possible to renew the certificate without receiving extra counseling.

It isn't just the homeowner who can request a counseling session. Someone with power of attorney can also qualify, as can a guardian or conservator. No one else has such a right—not even a relative.

What should you look for in a counselor?

- Someone with experience—maybe at least five years' worth. An experienced person should know how to deal with unusual situations.

- Someone who doesn't tell you what to do. Instead, the counselor should lay out the choices and then outline the pros and cons. If a homeowner might be moving in a year or two, the counselor will show that person how much higher the cost of a reverse mortgage will be. "I don't encourage or discourage anyone," says Stephen Pepe, a counselor. "Mine is not a do-or-don't role. I don't render opinions. If someone needs just a few thousand dollars right now, and only for a short time, I may talk about a home-improvement loan or a home-equity loan." Tyndal also recognizes that her job is not to sell reverse mortgages, even to people who she is sure would benefit: "Some people just have it in their hearts to save their home free and clear for their children, and it's hard for them to borrow money on their houses. I just try to make everything really simple for them to understand."
- Someone who seems knowledgeable—who gives persuasive answers to your questions, such as, "Why shouldn't I get a home-equity loan instead? How can I bring down closing costs?"
- Someone who comes recommended. Call a servicer like Wells Fargo, Seattle Mortgage, or Financial Freedom and ask for recommendations. People there are permitted to give five. The ones they have recommended to me, for interviews, have been top-notch.
- Someone who, on your first encounter, doesn't seem rushed and impatient.
- Someone who puts you so much at ease that you aren't afraid of asking "dumb" questions, such as, "Is this a scam?" "Will people come by all the time to check on my home?" "Would you recommend this for your mother?" (Tyndal's own answer to the last question: "I would have.") In any case, smart people can ask dumb questions.
- Someone who truly listens to you. "Sometimes," says Tyndal, "a reverse mortgage is not the best choice."

Try to talk to three counselors before deciding which one to zero in on unless it has been hard for you to get any appointment at all, which has been typical recently. In the real world today, says Tyndal, "Most people don't really go to more that one counselor—they put in calls to a lot of different counselors, and whoever gets back to them first is the one they go with. They basically just want to get the process moving."

The counselor's role is vital. You must depend on the counselor not only for advice on what to do, but also for help if there is trouble.

Here's advice from Isis Malagrino, a senior HECM counselor for Novadebt: "There are huge advantages to counseling in person; it's much easier for the homeowner to understand the material presented, and there is better communication. Unfortunately, not everyone drives, or lives near a counselor. Also, with age, there are mobility issues."

"There are also advantages to using local counselors," she goes on. "The biggest advantage is being able to see them face to face. And a local counselor may be aware of other resources available to the homeowner, such as special services and other options that are different from state to state, even county to county."

She also suggests that, when scheduling a counseling session, you ask the counselor to mail you information first so that you can study up on such things as projections of how much money you might receive, what the cost would be, and what would be left after five or ten years.

Not all counselors are on the level of Jeeves, Bertie Wooster's god-like butler. Thomas Scabareti has met counselors who don't even know the fundamental rules. He has even met counselors biased against reverse mortgages. "They come in all sorts of flavors," as he puts it.

His own mother-in-law was interested in a reverse mortgage and met with a counselor. When Scabareti spoke with her, she had changed her mind. No reverse mortgage for her! Why not? The counselor had told her that she could not sell her house for three years.

Scabareti phoned the counselor. No, what he had said was that she should *try* not to sell the house for three years. He faults the counselor for not having made things clear to his mother-in-law and for not checking that she had understood the basics.

Financial Planners

By and large, the best financial planners are certified financial planners, and the best of these are fee-only CFPs.

Anyone can call himself or herself a financial planner, and some people without credentials do. CPAs who have special training are personal financial specialists (PFSs), but the verdict on them is that they tend to know little about investing. Chartered financial consultants (ChFCs) tend to be insurance-oriented.

There are lazy and venal fee-only CFPs and superior commission-paid CFPs. But, other things being equal, go for the fee-only CFP, who will not be tempted to sell you expensive deferred variable annuities, or mutual funds with poor records and huge sales charges, just for the extra money. For the names of fee-only CFPs near you, call the National Association of Personal Financial Advisors at 800-366-2732 or go to www.NAPFA.org. For the names of CFPs in general, phone 800-322-4237 or go to www.fpanet.org.

Before hiring a planner, find out what his or her area of expertise is. You want a planner accustomed to dealing with older people and their retirement concerns, not just with young people worried about saving for college for their kids or buying their first homes. Just as you should not hire a criminal lawyer to write your will, don't hire a financial planner with a lot of experience in areas that don't match your needs.

Even with the guidance of a reverse-mortgage counselor, many borrowers can benefit from hiring a CFP. A CFP can answer such questions as: How should you invest your money? Are you spending too much or too little? Do you have enough insurance and the right kinds, including umbrella insurance (which protects you against liability lawsuits beyond your auto and homeowners policies)?

A financial planner can be the quarterback of your financial life, checking that your will is up to date; that your investments are sensibly split among stocks, bonds, and cash equivalents; and that your tax strategy meshes with your investment strategy. (Too many seniors, for example, are heavily into tax-exempt bonds despite their being in low, marginal tax brackets.)

In one respect, almost everyone without a professional money manager can benefit from a financial planner: having someone to look over your portfolio. Ordinary investors tend to make the same mistakes over and over: buying whatever securities have been shooting out all the lights lately, having a lopsided portfolio (too much in one industry, for example) instead of a diversified portfolio, having too much money invested in one stock, holding on to losers and selling winners, having too much (or too little) in the stock market, buying the wrong kinds of stocks (for most seniors, the right stocks are typically blue-chip dividend-payers, very likely inside a mutual fund).

Not long ago, one old woman asked a financial planner to look over her portfolio. Said the planner, Lauren Locker, CFP, of Totowa, New Jersey: "I see that you have a stockbroker. Why do you need me?" The old woman insisted. Locker found that the broker was not having the woman's dividends or interest reinvested in more mutual funds, as she should have; instead, the money was accumulating and then being used to buy something else—and thus give the broker another commission. Said the old woman, "My broker said I couldn't reinvest my money."

The broker was also buying mutual funds sponsored by his brokerage firm, which gave the broker higher-than-normal commissions. "My broker said he could buy only these funds," said the old woman.

Locker checked with the brokerage firm; yes, customers could reinvest their distributions, and, yes, they could buy funds other than Dean Witter funds.

"Why," Locker finally asked the old woman in exasperation, "have you been so trusting of your broker?"

Said the old woman, "He's my nephew."

Good financial planners are expensive. In upscale areas, the going rate in 2005 was $150 to $300 an hour, 1 percent of your portfolio for an entire financial plan, and 1 percent to manage your portfolio.

The Case for Hourly Planners

If you don't think you can afford a financial planner, you are far from being alone. One poll found that 46 percent of Americans say they cannot afford one; 42 say say either that they can or that they already have one; and 11 percent don't know.

The solution for people of modest means may be a planner who charges by the hour and not 1 percent of your assets to manage your portfolio and not a minimum of, say, $1,000.

Hourly planners are cheaper. One poll has found that hourly fees range from $50 to $375, with the median being $125. Traditional financial planners charge an average of a little less than $1,800 for help, with the median being $775. (*Solutions,* October 2005.)

An ideal person to consult an hourly planner has just one or two pressing questions, such as: Is my portfolio suitable for a person in my situation? Then again, you may want to give a financial planner a trial run just to see if he or she is any good.

I suggest to most people that they consider having an outsider who's smart look over their portfolio. Is it diversified enough? With U.S. stocks and foreign, small- and large-company stocks, growth and value stocks? Are there stinkers you should have abandoned long ago? Is your portfolio too aggressive (lots of over-the-counter stocks) or too conservative (lots of money in short-term bond funds)?

Sheryl Garrett, the high priestess of hourly planners, lives in Shawnee Mission, Kansas. She has trained 250 hourly planners around the country—and, recently, one in Thailand. For names of the planners Garrett trained who are near you, go to www.garrettplanning.network.com or phone 877-510-1500.

Another good thing about Garrett planners is that all of them are fee-only. Garrett began thinking of hourly planning for the less wealthy while she herself was working for a big financial planning firm. "I found myself having to turn away folks that I wanted to work with," she said. "It was emotionally disturbing that I couldn't work with people because they didn't have enough money to pay our minimum." (Garrett planners require no minimum payment.)

She was also vexed at having to recommend only those investments that paid commissions. A couple needed more cash; she couldn't tell them to stick more money into a money market fund that paid no commission. Five years ago, she launched her hourly, as-needed network.

Garrett planners typically spend five to ten hours with new clients at the first formal meeting and then two to four hours in a follow-up meeting. The range of fees, Garrett reported, is $150 to $300 per hour, "with a whole lot on the lower end."

Typical clients include people who need to know whether or not they are doing the right thing. There are also people with specific questions, such as: Am I saving enough for retirement? They are not what Garrett calls "wealthy delegators," rich people who can afford to pay others to do everything for them or to answer complex questions about (say) their stock options.

"For us, this isn't rocket science," she told me. "Most of our clients have straightforward situations. They don't have tax-planning problems. They have all-American issues."

Her hope for the future is that 75 to 85 percent of all financial advisers will be giving hourly advice, usually to people of modest income, "because this is where the need is."

Elder-Law Attorneys

A couple of older homeowners, overflowing with love for their children, signed their house over to them—lock, stock, barrel, and deed.

The kids, eager to get their hands on real money, proceeded to sell the house—without letting their parents know.

To keep from being evicted, the parents had to buy the house back from the new owners. And eventually, thanks to their elder-law attorney, they got the house-sale money back from their children.

That particular horror story was told by Donald M. McHugh, a certified elder-law attorney with McHugh & Macri in East Hanover, New Jersey, and chairman of the 400-member N.J. Bar Association elder-law section.

Elder-law attorneys have been getting a lot of attention of late, even though the elder/disability specialty has been around since 1982. The term "elder law" was coined in around 1988 when the National Academy of Elder Law Attorneys (NAELA) was formed.

Elder law is complex because it encompasses an enormous arena—any legal matters relating to the elderly. Some of these areas, as listed on the Web site of NAELA, include:

- Medicaid.
- Medicare claims and appeals.
- Income, estate, and tax planning.
- Preservation/transfer of assets to avoid spousal impoverishment when the other spouse enters a nursing home.
- Social Security and disability claims and appeals.

- Supplemental and long-term health insurance issues.
- Elder abuse and fraud-recovery cases.
- Age discrimination in employment.

An issue that elder-law attorneys confront frequently is how to prevent older people from getting wiped out. Says McHugh, "Ninety percent of my clients share the same concern: Is my nest egg at risk if I get sick? The bad news is that the answer is yes. The good news is that some but not all of the nest egg must be spent on health-care costs, but you can control how much." After they spend their fair share, they can access public programs like Medicaid.

McHugh became interested in elder-law 15 years ago after 20 years as a real estate and zoning lawyer. "I thought I knew everything—until my own mother had to go through the maze of health care. I knew nothing in this area." So he hit the books, passed the test, and then specialized. What was then a niche, he says, has grown into a vast practice area.

One reason there is such a specialty these days, McHugh explains, is that every decision that older people make with regard to their health care affects their finances—taxes, insurance issues, estate planning. Also, the area is extremely complex. Many referrals that elder-law attorneys get come from other lawyers, who belatedly discover that they have bitten off more than they can chew.

On the subject of gifts to children, McHugh says that although it may seem like a fine idea, "It could be the worst thing from the parents' point of view." If the parents surrender control and give their kids their house, they may wind up on the street. As for the children, the gift of a house can represent a time bomb. The parents may have bought a house for $29,900 that is now worth $500,000. Because of that $29,900 cost basis, whenever the kids sell, they would owe a capital-gains tax of around $70,000.

But, he points out, if the parents retain a life estate in the house (they could stay there for as long as they lived), the kids would inherit the house at a stepped-up basis of $500,000 and owe no tax.

While health-care costs may occupy elder-law attorneys in this area, Lawrence Davidow of Long Island, New York, president of the National Academy of Elder Care Lawyers, reports that different areas of the country have different specialties. It may be age discrimination, or questions of

Exhibit 7.1 10 Questions to Ask a Financial Planner

1. What experience have you had?
2. What are your qualifications? (What certifications does the person have?)
3. What services do you offer?
4. What is your approach to financial planning?
5. Will you be the only person working with me?
6. How will I pay for your services?
7. How much do you typically charge?
8. Could anyone besides me benefit from your recommendations? (Checking for conflicts of interest.)
9. Have you ever been publicly disciplined for any unlawful or unethical acts in your professional career?
10. Would you write out what services you will provide and what you will charge?

Source: Certified Financial Planner Board of Standards.

guardianship, or end-of-life decisions. "This is not an area for a generalist," he adds.

How to find a good elder-law attorney? Davidow suggests asking: Does the lawyer do real estate all day long, or criminal law, too? What predominates in his or her practice? How long has the lawyer been practicing elder law? Does he or she write or lecture on the subject?

Half of all elder-law attorneys, he reports, are hired by the older people themselves, the other half by their children.

The National Academy of Elder Law Attorneys has an informative Web site and lists elder-law attorneys around the country. Go to www.naela.com. Ten important questions to ask a financial planner are listed in Exhibit 7-1.

8

Decisions, Decisions

If you decide to obtain a reverse mortgage, you have quite a few important decisions to make and some questions to ask yourself. This chapter discusses four major questions.

1. *Do you want a term mortgage for a specific number of years or a tenure mortgage, one that continues until you leave the house or die? The second is far more common.*

With a term mortgage, payments stop on a specific date. It is not common. Borrowers may choose the fixed-term mortgage when they expect to be receiving money at a certain time in the future (perhaps from Social Security) and may no longer need a reverse mortgage. With a tenure mortgage, you can remain in the house as long as you wish, if you follow the rules

2. *Do you want a mortgage whose interest rate adjusts every month or every year?* Choosing the one that adjusts every year can help insulate you from interest-rate increases, but you get a larger loan with monthly charges.

Another choice you have with a HECM: an interest rate that adjusts every year and an interest rate that adjusts every month. There is no fixed-rate choice.

The yearly rate tracks the one-year U.S. Treasury security rate. The rate cannot go up, or down, by more than 2 percentage points in a year. And it cannot change by more than 5 percentage points, up or down, over the course of the loan. The limits on the upside protect you; the limits on the downside protect the lender.

The monthly rate tracks the rise or fall in the U.S. Treasury rate. It cannot change by more than 10 percentage points over the course of the loan.

Most people choose the monthly rate. You get a lower interest rate to start off with, and higher cash advances. One advantage of the yearly rate is that there are tighter restrictions on rises in interest rates. Another advantage: interest rate increases are slower to raise your own rate. A drawback: if rates fall, the interest rate will be slower to follow suit.

3. *How do you want to receive your money? As a lump sum? A line of credit? A monthly income? A combination of those three?* Most people choose a line of credit—money to pay the big bills, like property taxes, which might otherwise upend their budgets. A benefit of this choice is that you spend the value of your home, and owe interest, only when you decide you really need the money.

A danger with a line of credit is that if you spend too much, you may not have enough to pay for such necessities as your taxes and homeowner's insurance. To prevent this, have the lender regularly pay the property taxes and insurance out of your funds. That will, of course, lower your available credit because the lenders will keep money for these debts in reserve.

A monthly income is the choice of people who continually need money to pay their bills and, in general, to live comfortably. This is like an income annuity, but, unlike an annuity, it is not portable. If you leave the house, the payments end. Also, unlike an income annuity, you may be able to wangle a higher monthly payment later on. And, of course, unlike an annuity, the income you receive is not taxable.

Perhaps it would be best to choose a monthly income along with a credit line. That way, if rates go up, you can lock in a higher payment rate. Also, the credit line can act as an emergency fund in case you have unexpected expenses.

A lump sum might be the choice of people who have a one-time overwhelming need, such as making their home safer and more comfortable. You need not take out all the money available; you can leave what remains for other uses.

The Bank of New York's Joseph DeMarkey reports that a lump sum is the least popular choice and is suitable mainly for people with "a well-defined need." The money you earn on your lump sum, if you keep it in a safe place (like a money market fund), will be less than the interest you are charged. It can also make you ineligible for benefits available for seniors, like SSI.

Some people use a lump sum to buy an income or immediate annuity. Although the payments may be partly taxable, they never stop. And if you are not especially risk-averse, you could buy a variable-income annuity, which might have some exposure to the stock market (see Chapter 11). A possible choice is to buy an income annuity with some of the lump sum and also choose a monthly income. (You should probably avoid deferred annuities. See Chapter 16.)

A sensible combination would be a lump sum to pay off major obligations, and the remainder for either a line of credit or a monthly income.

4. *What kind of reverse mortgage do you want? A HECM? A Fannie Mae Home Keeper? Or a Cash Account mortgage?* In most cases, a HECM is best. The loan you will probably wind up with is a home equity conversion mortgage (HECM). More than 80 percent of reverse mortgages issued are HECMs. This mortgage is backed by the U.S. Department of Housing and Urban Development and is insured by the Federal Housing Administration (FHA) so that you can never owe more than your house is worth. You can get a HECM from mortgage companies or banks. (See Chapter 9 for more details.)

HUD's reverse mortgages have limits on how much you can borrow. The limits are there to confine reverse mortgages to people in need of some extra money, but not a whole lot of money. They are for John Doe, not John D. Rockefeller. If you have a $5 million house, you won't get more of a loan than someone with a $300,000 house (in your area).

Every county in the country has its own limits. and the more upscale the county, the higher the 203-b limit, as it's called. The reason is that an average home in Beverly Hills costs far more than an average home in East St. Louis. But the limit is not the amount you can borrow; you might be able to borrow 50 or 60 percent of the limit.

Fannie Mae offers a Home Keeper reverse mortgage, which has not proved popular. But it gives you the interesting option of using your loan to buy another house.

State and local governments also offer reverse mortgages, but usually (a) they must be used for just one purpose, such as repairing your house or paying your property taxes, (b) they are for relatively small amounts, and (c) they are available only to homeowners in financial need. You can learn about such mortgages through your reverse mortgage counselor.

Reverse mortgages offered by private, profit-making companies like Financial Freedom are the most expensive. But you can borrow more money through such a "proprietary" reverse mortgage than through a HECM. For a list of proprietary reverse-mortgage lenders, go to www.reversemortgage.org, which is maintained by the National Reverse Mortgage Lenders Association.

If you home is worth $500,000 or more, you might consider a reverse mortgage issued by a private company like Financial Freedom. The costs will be higher than with a HECM, but, like a HECM, it will be insured so that you cannot owe more than whatever your house turns out to be worth.

If you know that you will sell and move in a few years, you could get an uninsured mortgage, which is available in Arizona, California, Massachusetts, and Minnesota. It will be less expensive than a traditional reverse mortgage because you won't be paying for insurance.

Summaries of the features of these reverse mortgages are in Exhibits 8.1–8.3, which follow.

Exhibit 8.1 Highlights of the FHA-HECM (Home Equity Conversion Mortgage)

- Maximum lending limit: $312,894 (in 2005).
- Limit depends on area of the country and the value of house.
- Homes that qualify: single-family detached; condominium; manufactured home; planned unit development; one–four rental unit if one is owner-occupied.
- Government insurance so debt cannot exceed house value.
- 2 percent up-front mortgage insurance premium; can be financed by loan.
- Available to homeowners aged 62 or older.
- No income requirements.
- Interest rate is adjusted monthly or yearly.
- Monthly: lifetime cap of 10 percent; annually: 5 percent cap.
- Rate is T-bill interest rate plus margin for profit.
- Payments: a lump sum, a line of credit, monthly income, or a combination.
- Proceeds are not taxable.
- Borrower can use proceeds without restriction (except for paying for advice about reverse mortgages).
- Balance on line of credit increases every year.
- You can choose a limit on the mortgage length ("term") or until you leave ("tenure").
- Closing and loan-origination costs can be paid by the loan.
- A $30 yearly servicing fee is added to the balance.
- Does not affect Social Security/Medicare eligibility.
- Consultation with an approved HUD counselor is required.
- Loan is due when home is no longer primary residence.

Exhibit 8.2 Home Keeper by Fannie Mae

- Maximum lending limit: $359,650 (2005).
- Homes that qualify: single-family detached; condominium; planned unit development; one–four rental unit if one is owner-occupied.
- Available to homeowners age 62 or over.
- No income requirements.
- Interest rate is adjusted monthly—CD rate plus profit margin.
- Payments: a lump sum, a line of credit.
- Proceeds are not taxable.
- Closing and loan-origination costs can be paid by loan.
- A $35 monthly service fee is added to the balance.
- Does not affect Social Security/Medicare eligibility.
- No limit on use of proceeds.
- Proceeds can be used to purchase a home.
- No mortgage insurance and no mortgage insurance premium.
- Lifetime cap of 12 percent over initial rate.
- Consultation with an approved Fannie Mae or HUD counselor is required.
- Loan is due when home is no longer primary residence.

Exhibit 8.3 Financial Freedom Cash Account

General provisions, followed by three options:

- For homeowners age 62 or older.
- No maximum loan limit or home value.
- Eligible houses start at $500,000.
- Homes that qualify: single-family detached; condominium; planned unit development, one–four rental unit if one is owner-occupied; cooperatives in New York State.
- Interest rate is six-month LIBOR plus 5 percent margin; cap is 6 percent.
- Proceeds are not taxable.
- No prepayment penalty.
- No equity or appreciation sharing, no maturity fee.
- Consultation with an independent counselor required
- Service fee is financed monthly.
- Loan cannot exceed value of house ("nonrecourse").
- No repayment until borrower permanently moves out of house.

Option 1: Simply Zero

- No origination fee.
- At closing, borrower must draw all of the maximum loan available.
- No closing costs (apart from local or state taxes).
- No prepayment penalty.
- Full repayment permitted, but partial not allowed first five years.
- Adjustable rate; six-month LIBOR plus 5 percent profit. Reset every six months.

Option 2: Zero Point

- No origination fee.
- At closing, borrower must draw of 75 percent of the maximum loan available.
- Minimum draw is $500.
- Unused line of credit grows by 5 percent a year.
- Closing costs are actual third-party costs, not to exceed $3,500 (excluding local or state taxes).

(Continued)

Exhibit 8.3 (*Continued*)

- No prepayment penalty.
- Full prepayment permitted, but partial prepayment not permitted on minimum draw for first five years.
- Interest rate is six-month LIBOR plus 5 percent profit. Reset every six months.

Option 3: Standard

- Origination fee is maximum of 2 percent of loan value.
- Revolving line of credit is open-ended.
- Unused line of credit grows by 5 percent a year.
- Minimum draw is $500.
- Interest rate is six-month LIBOR plus 5 percent profit. Rate reset every six months.

9

Choosing a
Mortgage:
The HECM

In most cases, a Home-Equity Conversion Mortgage will be the best choice for you, and it is the loan you will probably wind up getting. It's called a HECM—pronounced "hehcum." More than 80 percent of reverse mortgages issued are HECMs.

This mortgage is backed by the U.S. Department of Housing and Urban Development (HUD) and insured by the Federal Housing Administration (FHA) so that you can never owe more than your house is worth.

If your home is worth $500,000 or more, you might consider a reverse mortgage issued by a private company, like Financial Freedom. The cost will be higher than the cost with a HECM, but, like a HECM it will be insured so that you cannot owe more than whatever your house turns out to be worth. And you can borrow more money with such a "proprietary" reverse mortgage than you can with a HECM. For a list of proprietary reverse-mortgage lenders, go to www.reversemortgage.org, which is maintained by the National Reverse Mortgage Lenders Association.

HUD's reverse mortgages have limits on how much you can borrow. The limits are there to confine reverse mortgages to people in need of some extra money. In fact, every county in the country has its own limits, and the wealthier the county, the higher the limit.

This chapter describes the HECM; the next is devoted to the Home Keeper, and the chapter after that to Financial Freedom's Cash Account. A summary of their features can be found in the exhibits at the end of Chapter 8.

The money you obtain from a HECM can be spent any way you wish, apart from paying someone to give you advice about a reverse mortgage. HECMs are available in Puerto Rico and the District of Columbia, along with all 50 states.

Who Is Eligible?

You and anyone else applying for a HECM must be 62 years of age or older. You must live in the home, and it must be your principal residence, not a weekend or summer home.

Cooperatives (except in New York City) and most mobile homes are excluded. Acceptable are single-family residences, units in a one–to-four unit development or part of a planned unit development, and a cooperative approved by HUD.

Before applying for a reverse mortgage, you must talk with a HUD-approved counselor from a HUD-approved agency. You must obtain a certificate before applying for the loan.

How Much You Will Receive

The amount of your loan depends on:

1. How old you and the other borrowers are. The older you are, the more money you will receive because an older person is less likely to live as long as a younger person, and thus the loan is likely to be repaid sooner. If there is more than one borrower, the age of the youngest one is used.
2. How valuable the house is. While there are limits for every county in the country, the limits tend to go up every year. If your house is valued at $300,000 and the limit in your county is $200,000, your loan will be based on $200,000. You would receive a percentage of that $200,000 as a loan.

3. The interest rate. The higher it is, the less you will receive.

4. How you decide to have the loan paid to you.

Receiving the Loan

You have four choices of how to receive the money:

1. A lump sum.

2. A line of credit. You decide when and how much you wish to withdraw. This is, sensibly, the most popular choice.

3. A monthly income for as long as you live in the home; this is a "tenure" plan.

4. A monthly income for a certain period of time, perhaps until you come into money you are expecting. This is called a "term" plan.

You can also choose a combination of these options—both a line of credit and a monthly income, for example, although both of these will be for lower amounts. For $20, you can change your payment plan at any time.

Suggestions on which to choose are provided in Chapter 8.

How Much You Will Receive

For an estimate of how much of a HECM loan you might receive, check with the calculators available online or ask a counselor. One calculator is at www.aarp.org/revmort.

A special benefit of the credit-line option is that it grows larger every month because of the interest rate being charged on your loan.

Repayment Time

A loan will become due:

- If all borrowers move out to another permanent residence.
- If the last remaining borrower does not live in the house for 12 consecutive months, even if this is caused by illness.
- If the house deteriorates (beyond ordinary wear and tear) and the homeowner doesn't make repairs.
- If the homeowner doesn't pay the property taxes and homeowner's insurance.

You normally have 12 months to repay the loan.

Paying the Piper

The closing costs of a HECM, unfortunately, shock some borrowers. (The closing is when the mortgage goes into effect—when the deal is closed.)

But bear in mind: These are mostly one-time costs. If you live in the house for several years, spreading out the expense, those costs are not so formidable.

You can add the costs of a HECM to the loan itself—in a sense, finance them. That leaves you with more cash, which is nice, but lowers the amount of money in the loan available to you.

A summary of the major expenses follows.

Third Party Costs. These are the debts you owe to third parties and not to the lender. They include the cost of an appraisal, a title search (to make sure the property is owned free and clear), title insurance (to protect the lender), surveys, recording fees, mortgage taxes, credit checks, home inspection, and so forth. Some of these expenses can be lowered if you bargain. (See Chapter 14.)

Origination Fee. You pay the lender for originating the loan—the paperwork and processing. You will pay 2 percent of your home's value or 2 percent of your county's 203-b limit, whichever is less. But if the amount is less than $2,000, the lender can charge $2,000. This is an expense where you can haggle with lenders. Get three bids.

Mortgage Insurance Premium. This is the insurance that covers a situation in which the house turns out to be worth less than the loan, or the lender cannot fulfill his or her obligations. No, the insurance is not for making a profit.

There are two parts to the fee:

1. 2 percent of your home's appraised value or the 203-b limit in your county, whichever is lower.
2. 0.5 percent is added to the interest rate you are charged—five "basis points."

Servicing Fee. This cost is limited to $30 a month for annually adjustable interest rates and to $35 for monthly adjustable rates. Lenders may charge less. The yearly cost may thus be $360 or $420, so shop around. Servicing

Exhibit 9.1 Monthly or Annually?

Monthly adjustable:
- Larger loans.
- Rates will be lower than annual adjustable when increases in the T-rate are less than 2.6 percentage points a year, or 5.6 points over the life of the loan.
- Your rate can decrease by over 2 points a year, over 5 points over the life of the loan.
- If rates fall, the monthly adjustable rate will fall sooner than the annually adjustable rate.

Annually adjustable:
- Lower rate when T-rate increases are over 2.6 points a year, 5.6 points over the life of the loan.
- If rates increase, the annually adjustable rate will rise more slowly than the monthly adjustable rate.

includes making loan advances when you ask for them, sending the insurance premiums to the FHA, sending you account statements, and so forth.

Interest Rates. Lenders offer an adjustable-rate mortgage tied to the one-year U.S. Treasury security rate. So the rate can change once a year. But the changes are limited to two percentage points a year and five total points over the life of the loan.

The borrower can choose instead an adjustable-rate mortgage that changes every month. This rate will be lower, but it can go to a maximum of 10 percentage points over the life of the loan. See Exhibit 9.1.

On top of the interest rate is a margin for profit set by Fannie Mae.

Total Annual Loan Cost. Every lender must give you an estimate of what the reverse mortgage will cost per year, the total annual loan cost (TALC). But this estimate is just that—an estimate. No one knows how long you will live in the house, and the longer you live there, the lower the annual costs will be. No one knows where interest rates will go. And even the borrower may not know in advance how or when he or she will use the credit line. Even so, because lenders use the same formula, comparing the TALC rates offered by different lenders is a good idea.

10

Choosing a Mortgage: Fannie Mae Home Keeper

The Fannie Mae Home Keeper Mortgage is similar to HUD's home-equity conversion mortgage (HECM), but it is different in several important ways. Among them:

- For average or above-average valued homes, you may qualify for a higher line of credit or higher monthly income payment. The maximum lending limit in 2005 was $359,650, almost $50,000 more than HECM's limit.
- Interest rates are usually higher, but the fees are lower.
- You do not pay for mortgage insurance, although Fannie Mae guarantees that you will receive your reverse-mortgage money even if the lender cannot pay you.
- You can use the proceeds to buy a new house—the Home Keeper for Home Purchase Loan. This interesting option is covered at the end of this chapter.
- The popularity of the Home Keeper is nowhere near the level of the HECM. Several counselors report that rarely, in fact, does any borrower obtain more money with a Home Keeper than with a

HECM. One reverse-mortgage counselor, with several years of experience, reports that he has never seen a client wind up with a Home Keeper.

- Several authorities believe that the Home Keeper will eventually be changed to offer a greater choice to borrowers, and the most likely change will be a sharply higher increase in the permissible loan amount. (For more information, call 800-732-6643 or visit www.fanniemae.com.)
- Fannie Mae started life as a government agency (called the Federal National Mortgage Association), but went private in 1968. Its stock is listed on the New York Stock Exchange. (The price is down because of accounting irregularities.) Its main job remains buying mortgages from lenders, thus providing lenders with a regular supply of new money to make new mortgage loans.
- How much can you borrow? That depends on:
  - Your age and the age of your co-borrowers (if there are three, the average of the two lower ages is used).
  - The appraised value of your property.
  - The "adjusted property value."

Like the HECM, the Fannie Mae has a limit (called a "principal limit") on the amount you can borrow, but it is calculated differently from the way the HECM is calculated.

The limit is based on the average house price in the United States. Your principal limit will be the lower of either (1) the average house price in the country or (2) your actual appraised property value. So, if your house is appraised at $310,000 and the Fannie Mae loan limit is $359,650, you will qualify for $310,000. (A much simpler calculation than the HECM, which focuses on local house prices throughout the country.)

Naturally, if two or more people are coborrowers, they will receive less of a loan than one person would. The chances of at least one person in a couple enjoying a long life are better than the chances of just one of them living a long time.

To receive the money, you can choose:

- The tenure plan, in which your loan continues until you leave the house, die, or break the rules.

- A line of credit, but, unlike the HECM, the line of credit doesn't grow (not available in Texas).
- A modified tenure plan, in which you receive a monthly income as well as a line of credit. (Naturally, the monthly income will be lower if you did not have funds in a line of credit.) You can decide, within limits, how much you want in monthly income and how much in a line of credit. This is a smart option for conservative people.

A lump-sum option, though not widely known, may also be available.

You can change your choices whenever you like, but may be charged up to $50 to make a change. You can add a line of credit to a tenure plan; add a monthly payment to a line of credit; and convert to a line of credit from a tenure plan.

If you decide you don't need regular monthly payments, you can suspend them at any time, and you can have them resume at any time. This would be a good move if you might otherwise be disqualified from receiving Social Security income or Medicaid payments.

As with all reverse mortgages, the interest rate is adjustable. The Home Keeper's rate is based on the secondary market CD plus a margin for profit; the maximum is 3.4 percent. So, if the one-month CD rate is 2 percent, your interest rate might be a maximum of 5.4 percent.

Because the CD is monthly, your rate will change monthly. There is a 12 percentage point cap on the rate over the loan's lifetime. So, if your interest began at 5 percent, it will never exceed 17 percent. You can check the current rate by going to www.federalreseve.gov/releases/h15/current.

The expenses include the origination fee, which in this case cannot be more than $2,000 or 2 percent of the adjusted property value, whichever is more. (It can be paid out of your loan at the closing.) Other expenses include a monthly servicing fee (capped at $30) plus other closing costs such as for a title search and insurance, appraisal, credit report, termite inspection, and so forth. Fannie Mae permits all closing costs to be tucked into your loan balance, although some lenders insist that borrowers pay cash for the cost of appraisals and home inspections—whatever is done by third parties.

Other rules that govern reverse mortgages in general include:

- Your loan comes due when the last co-borrower dies, if you or the last surviving co-borrower move out (you have not lived in the home as your primary residence for most of the year), if you sell the home, if you do not maintain the property, if you do not pay the property taxes or homeowner's insurance.

- You have three days to cancel the loan after you have signed a contract. These three days include Saturdays but not Sundays and holidays. Your money will not be available until after this three-day rescission period.

- Residences that qualify: single-family houses, condominiums, town houses, manufactured housing, cooperatives, two- to four-unit properties.

- You must receive counseling from a non-profit HUD counselor or a Fannie Mae counselor. This can take place in person or over the phone. The counselor will estimate the payments you can receive and your likely costs, will compare the Home Keeper with other reverse-mortgage options, and so forth.

- You must be age 62 or over, and the home must be your primary residence. Three co-borrowers are permissible, nonrelated, but all must be 62 or over. Typically they are parents and an adult child. (More than three people can live in the house, of course, but for a reverse mortgage the names of only three people can be on the title.)

- You must own your home outright or have only a small mortgage balance, which you can pay off at the closing with a cash advance.

- If your home needs repairs, you can complete them after your reverse mortgage closes, and money for them will be held in your line of credit. Usually the repairs must be completed within six months.

- Your balance includes the amount you owe, interest, and other expenses that you did not pay in cash at the closing (origination fees, for example).

- You can pay all or part of your loan balance without penalty. If you do, your line of credit will increase and your balance will shrink. If you direct that the payment go toward interest and not principal, you may be able to deduct the interest from your taxes (if you can itemize your deductions).

- Fannie Mae will allow Home Keeper mortgages for homes held in trust.

Maybe you want to buy a smaller home, or a home nearer your friends and family, or a home easier for an older person to get around in, or a home in a warmer climate. You may even want a larger, more expensive home, although David Carey, senior product manager of the Home Keeper, reports that most people buy a smaller house. At the same time, you could definitely use more money to live on.

You might then consider a special feature that the Fannie Mae offers— help in buying a different home. You can wind up with a different home and no mortgage payments without depleting all your other assets. And you can have a reverse mortgage on the new home. The benefits here are speed and simplicity, no new mortgage payments, and only one closing.

But to buy the new home, you must make a small down payment and reveal where the money came from. Gifts are acceptable. (The older you are, the smaller the down payment. With someone young, the lender would normally have to spend a longer period of time servicing the loan.) A reverse mortgage is intended to cover the remainder, although your savings may cover it. (You cannot get another mortgage on your new house.)

The general rules are largely the same as those with the Home Keeper with respect to costs, repayments, and interest rate. Manufactured houses, some planned unit developments, and some condos are acceptable. You must have a counseling session with an approved counselor.

Some differences between this and the Home Keeper include:

- There is no three-day right of rescission.
- The money from your new reverse mortgage will be available only as a line of credit, not as a monthly income or lump sum.
- At the closing, the appraised value of your property will determine the size of your loan, not the actual sales price. So the size of the loan may be calculated on a figure higher or lower than the actual sales price.

- You must start living in your new home within 30 days of the date of the closing.

Deciding whether to use the Home Keeper for Purchase Loan or just to sell your house and buy another with the proceeds is complex, and you should ask your advisers for guidance. But with the Home Keeper for Purchase, you have only one closing. And it allows you to buy a new home, something you may not do with a HECM.

11

Getting a Mortgage: The Jumbo Cash Account

Can you obtain a reverse mortgage if your house is worth $18 million? A woman in California did. She got a jumbo cash account.

Cash accounts are mainly for people who own expensive houses—those valued at $500,000 or over—not for people who need to scrape up money to pay their everyday bills. The leading company that makes cash-account reverse mortgages (and, in fact, that invented the idea) is Financial Freedom of Irvine, California, which gave the loan to the woman with the $18 million house. The average house that it provides a cash-account reverse mortgage for is valued at $1.2 million to $1.4 million.

Why would people not suffering financially want a reverse mortgage? Joseph Mahoney, CEO of Financial Freedom, notes that these people may simply need liquidity—cash. And perhaps they don't want to sell their stocks because the stocks are in the basement now or selling them would trigger huge capital-gains taxes, or because the stocks seem poised to go up. They don't want to sell their bonds because they need the income the bonds throw off. And when they examine their portfolios, they conclude that much too much of their worldly wealth is in a single house—perhaps more than half.

Getting a loan against your house doesn't reduce your real-world exposure to real estate (you still own the house), but if your house serves as collateral, it is not quite the same as an ordinary house. This can also lower the estate taxes of someone who is very wealthy.

Perhaps the owners also want to put that somnolent money to better use, such as to buy a new business, to make gifts to their children or pay for the educations of their grandchildren, to pay income taxes and property taxes now, to pay any estate taxes after they die. Even the well-to-do can be exceedingly house-rich and, if not cash-poor, then cash-deficient.

They may also make lifestyle choices, Mahoney said, traveling more, buying another home, making their own home more "senior-friendly," living a more luxurious life in general.

Besides, Mahoney points out, these days having a very expensive house does not necessarily make you all that rich. On the East and West Coasts, a house that people bought for $30,000 in 1960 may be worth $1 million now, and yet their income probably has not climbed by such leaps and bounds. "Their income may be under pressure from medical bills and the high cost of living in general," he pointed out. So they, too, may need a reverse mortgage to pay their everyday bills.

With a Financial Freedom cash account, you can usually borrow more money than with other reverse mortgages, but you will pay a higher interest rate. Do you want more money now and less money later on?

For moderately priced homes, usually you will do better with a HECM or Home Keeper, getting more money at a lower cost.

For a comparison, go to www.financialfreedom.com/calculator/imput.asp and fill in the blanks—age, value of home, zip code, any debts.

Other companies offer these jumbo loans for reverse mortgages, but they tend to operate in only a few larger states. They are called "proprietary" loans because private corporations offer them—not the government, as with the HECM.

Financial Freedom was founded as recently as 1996, in Irvine, California, and it is owned by a nationwide mortgage lender, IndyMac Bank. It offers reverse mortgages in all 50 states. The company is a member of the National Reverse Mortgage Lenders Association, a good sign.

Mahoney, a friendly and intelligent man, notes the difficulties in competing with a government product like the HECM, which is most generous to its borrowers. HUD expects a couple to live to the same age as an individual, so the couple can borrow as much as an individual; whereas in the real world, a couple typically will outlive an individual (the couple gets two chances), so Financial Freedom will lend the couple less money than HECM will.

He is also justifiably proud of Financial Freedom's proprietary software, which permits a neat comparison among the different loans. "And we're indifferent to which reverse mortgage people choose," he said.

Financial Freedom's reverse mortgages are in many ways like the HECM and the Home Keeper. Borrowers must meet with HUD-approved or other trained counselors, for example. And they must be age 62 or older, have a house they live in full time, one not mortgaged to the hilt. The amount of the loan depends, as usual, on the value of the home, current interest rates, and the borrower's age. Typically it's 40 percent of the value of the home.

Residences that qualify include: a single-family home, condominium, manufactured home, planned unit development, one-to-four unit rental property (you live in one), or a cooperative in New York state.

In some key ways, the Financial Freedom cash account is different:

- You can obtain only a line of credit. You cannot receive monthly payments as long as you live in the house.
- The house must be worth a minimum of $75,000.
- Most of its programs require a withdrawal of at least $500.

Besides your being able to get a larger loan, cash accounts have other benefits:

- *Flexibility.* You can withdraw $500 and then increase your withdrawal rate the next month. Or you may not take anything. You can prepay your loan.
- *No prepayment penalty.* (This applies to all loans.)
- *Growth.* Your cash account (what you can borrow) grows at a rate of 5 percent a year.

There are three different types of cash accounts, and they are very different. Here's what they have in common:

- Almost no loan limit.
- The six-month LIBOR is the index for the adjustable-rate loan, plus a markup of 5 percentage points. (See below.)
- No mortgage insurance, although the loan is nonrecourse; that is, the lender cannot recover more than the value of the house, even if the loan exceeds the value.
- $30 a month servicing fee.
- A second appraisal is needed for properties valued at over $2 million.

Here's how the three different cash accounts differ:

The Standard Cash Account. This is the only one of the three cash accounts that has an origination fee, but it's the most flexible option. The origination fee is up to 2 percent of the value of the home for the first $500,000. Over $500,000, add 1.5 percent. Over $1 million, add 1 percent. For a home valued at $1.5 million, the origination fee would be $22,500 ($10,000 plus $7,500 plus $5,000).

The closing costs include the usual—title insurance, application fee, survey, and so forth.

You can borrow money, put some back, and borrow it again; it's an open-ended line of credit. You can prepay any amount at any time.

Zero Point Option. There are no up-front origination fees—hence the name, Zero Point. But there are closing costs, which are capped at up to $3,500.

You must withdraw up to 75 percent of your account right off the bat. After that you can withdraw the $500 minimum.

You can't prepay the initial loan for five years, but you can repay the entire loan at any time. (So the lender doesn't lose money on you.)

Simply Zero. For this cash account there is zero origination fee and zero closing costs.

You must withdraw 100 percent of your account right off the bat. You can't prepay the initial draw for five years, but you can repay the entire loan at any time. (So the lender doesn't lose money on you.) And no prepayments are allowed for five years. This is for people who need or want a lot of money right away, and not surprisingly it is the most popular First Financial cash-account option.

LIBOR stands for London InterBank Offered Rate, and it's an average of what foreign banks charge one another for big loans. It's a fast-moving index, quickly changing in line with market conditions, but the six-month index gives borrowers some breathing room. Many U.S. banks use this index. The cash account has a lifetime cap of 6 percentage points above the original interest rate.

For new borrowers, Financial Freedom offers a lower rate for the first six months—the six-month LIBOR index plus 4.5 percentage points, not 5 percentage points.

If you are approved for a Financial Freedom loan, you might go to a lender who is affiliated with the company, a "correspondent lender." The lender will be familiar with Financial Freedom's various mortgages.

Financial Freedom does offer HECM and Home Keeper reverse mortgages, too—a great many of them.

Financial Freedom's phone number is 888-738-3773. Its Web site is www.financialfreedom.com.

12

Looking for the Right Lender

Do you want a local lender or a national lender?

A national lender will service its own loans, which might lead to fewer snafus and more efficiency. But a local lender may have better contacts and be able to direct special breaks your way.

Says Bill Agner, "I have title insurance arrangements, so I can save people on closing costs. And because the only collateral for the loan is the home, I'm particular about appraisals. I dot the I's and cross the T's. And with my cheery disposition, I may be able to work my way through the system. All in all, I'm comfortable that I'm pretty knowledgeable to help people."

Local lenders assign their reverse mortgages to servicers, who do all the follow-up work, and typically they are the national lenders. If you do use a local lender, inquire which servicer or servicers the lender works with, and ask for samples of the documents the servicer will send to you.

Beyond the question of whether to use a local or a national lender is the question of the individuals you will deal with. Your counselor may be able to get you good lenders.

Says Jeff Taylor of Wells Fargo: "We find that people with a passion for the product are best. They have a sincere desire to help seniors."

Thomas Scabareti suggests paying more attention to the individual than to the company. "Lenders have only so such control over the product. Look for an individual who is patient and explains everything, and talk to a few of them."

Sarah Hulbert of Seattle Mortgage advises doing some research on the lender. Check with the Better Business Bureau and state agencies to make sure that the lender has a good reputation. How long has the lender been in business? Does the lender answer telephone questions in a reasonable amount of time? Will the loan officer come to your house?

Joseph DeMarkey of the Bank of New York Mortgage suggests getting recommendations from advisers you trust—perhaps someone at a local bank. But you might give special consideration to the question of closing costs, he notes. Sometimes you can save as much as a thousand dollars, especially in competitive areas, which tend to be urban rather than rural.

Joseph Mahoney, CEO of Financial Freedom, suggests that you make sure that any lender you use belongs to the Reverse Mortgage Lenders Association, which insists that its members adhere to a special code of conduct.

Naturally, a lender should be "experienced and knowledgeable about reverse mortgages, so can help the borrower tailor the loan to the borrower's needs," says Mahoney. Financial Freedom, like many other lenders, has special software that compares mortgages and makes projections as to costs. "Ours is the most complete," he insists.

Questions You Might Ask

You should know the answers to the following questions from having spoken to a reverse mortgage counselor, but sometimes you might ask questions just to confirm that the person you are interviewing knows his or her onions, or to check how clearly that person can answer a question. Here are sample questions, some of which the proper answer to is, "It depends."

How much money can I borrow on my house? (It depends.)

Will anything be left for my children? (Possibly.)

If my spouse dies, or if I die, will the other one have to move out? (No.)

Are there penalties if I pay off the mortgage early? (No.)

If I go to a nursing home, will the loan become due? (It depends on how long you are in the nursing home.)

Will this mortgage keep me from ever getting Medicaid or other public help? (It depends.)

Should I get a home-equity loan instead? (It depends.)

What will the closing costs be? (You should get an estimate.)

How can I lower the closing costs?

Which servicer do you use—and why?

In choosing a lender or originator for a HECM, AARP recommends that you look at the following:

1. Cost
2. Origination services
3. Loan servicing
4. The lender's commitment to meeting your needs

Two expenses that lenders control are (1) the origination fee and (2) the servicing fee. Check what each lender will charge you, and check out the cost of appraisals and title insurance, too, although the lender doesn't control these.

You also want to know how long a lender has been in the business. An experienced person can deal with unexpected problems and probably has a good relationship with the local HUD people (assuming you are obtaining a HECM). A good lender will not give you the impression that he or she is rushed; you will feel that you have plenty of time to ask questions, and you won't be embarrassed if you must admit you did not understand something the first time. Many lenders will visit you at your home. For the names of HUD-approved lenders, go to www.hud.gov/offices/hsg/sfh/hecm/hecmhome.cfm.

The Big Four

The descriptions of the largest servicers and originators of reverse mortgages provided in the following paragraphs come mainly from their official home pages on the Web. Whether Wells Fargo or Financial Freedom is the largest depends on which measurement you use.

Wells Fargo (877-937-9357)

Wells Fargo Home Mortgage is one of the nation's top retail mortgage lenders and one of the top lenders to both low-to-moderate-income customers and ethnic minorities. It is also one of the country's leading servicers of home mortgages. It operates the country's largest mortgage network from nearly 2,400 mortgage and Wells Fargo banking stores and the Internet. Based in Des Moines, Iowa, it services loans for over 5 million customers nationwide.

Wells Fargo Home Mortgage is also one of the leading originators of reverse mortgages in the nation, helping homeowners age 62 and older capitalize on the equity they have built in their homes to secure financial independence and peace of mind. In 2004, Wells Fargo Home Mortgage helped senior Americans secure over one-third of all reverse mortgages originated in the country.

Financial Freedom (888-REVERSE)

More seniors have chosen Financial Freedom than any other lender for their reverse mortgages. Here are a number of good reasons why you should join them.

Proven Leadership

Our management was instrumental in the development of the reverse mortgage concept in the United States back in the early 1990s. Today, we're the nation's largest reverse mortgage lender, having helped tens of thousands of seniors enjoy the benefits of this important financial tool.

Specialization

Financial Freedom focuses exclusively on reverse mortgages. We do not sell any other financial products. Our commitment has resulted in a level of experience and expertise that no other company can match.

Commitment to Education

Financial Freedom has found that education—making sure seniors understand exactly what a reverse mortgage is, and what it isn't—is critical to creating solutions for our senior customers and is the hallmark of success for our company. All of our efforts, from our brochures to our Web site to the professionalism of our representatives, are aimed at giving you the facts you need to make a smart decision about whether a reverse mortgage is right for you.

BNY Mortgage CoA Bank of New York Company (800-269-6797)

As the independently operated mortgage affiliate of The Bank of New York, the nation's oldest bank, BNY Mortgage is the fourth largest originator of reverse mortgage loans in the United States. BNY is a recognized leader in both innovative and consumer-oriented reverse mortgage loan products for America's senior homeowners.

Currently, BNY offers reverse mortgage loans in 10 states from Maine to Florida. Please call them for more information on this unique mortgage product specifically designed to help senior homeowners live a more comfortable and secure life.

Seattle Mortgage Company (800-233-4601)

Seattle Mortgage Company is the third largest originator and servicer of reverse mortgages in the United States, and one of two servicers equipped to sponsor other lenders to offer the HECM and Home Keeper products. Seattle Mortgage has been originating and servicing reverse mortgages since 1995, and it is a national company with retail and wholesale representation in all 50 states.

Seattle Mortgage, a subsidiary of Seattle Savings Bank, was established in 1944. The organization is the oldest independent mortgage banker in the Northwest and remains locally owned and family operated. Our over 500 employees include many influential leaders in local, state, and national mortgage banking organizations, including the Mortgage Bankers Association and the National Reverse Mortgage Lenders Association.

With over 60 years of independent mortgage banking experience, Seattle Mortgage is a pioneer in the reverse mortgage industry. Recently

The Reverse Mortgage Advantage

named the Best Large Family Business in the Pacific Northwest, the company strives to exceed the expectations of customers through innovation. Seattle Mortgage is continually adding to its list of products and services to accommodate all types of borrowers.

Both a retail and wholesale lender of reverse mortgages, the organization is a pioneer and a nationwide leader for this program, offering financial security and superior customer service to its senior homeowners.

13

Getting a Reverse Mortgage–Step by Step

Here is a simple guide to what you should do to obtain a reverse mortgage.

1. *Do your homework.* If you don't have access to the Internet, go to a public library and if necessary ask a librarian for help. (Appendix 3 contains information regarding some useful Web sites.)

Read different sources on reverse mortgages. Sometimes it takes a while for things to sink in. Use a mortgage calculator to find out how much you might borrow.

Call AARP at 800-434-3410 for a free copy of its publication "Home Made Money." You can also order it online at www.aarp.org/revmort.

Jack Guttentag, the gray eminence of the mortgage field, urges people not to delay unnecessarily. "Procrastinating on a reverse mortgage is easy because, unlike the situation when you took your first forward mortgage, you already have shelter and the children are grown and out," he writes. "Fight the tendency by making an informed decision, which could be that a reverse mortgage is not for you, or that it is for you but that it would be better to wait and allow the amount you can draw to rise."

I am not sure that he is right. Guttentag believes that a key reason why reverse mortgages have not become more common is that people procrastinate. But there can be good reasons for delay. Perhaps a home-equity loan would be better. Or selling the house to the children. And what if one spouse is not 62 yet? Should you take that person's name off the title? Dangerous.

Robert Preston, a financial planner in Danbury, Connecticut, advises his clients not to take out a reverse mortgage until they are in their late 70s, when they will receive a bigger loan and have a better idea of their financial situation.

But it may just be a question of semantics. Delay, yes; procrastinate, no.

Assuming you are eligible, determine how much money you can draw and what the mortgage will cost. You can do that by using an online calculator at one of the following Web sites: www.rmaarp.com, www.revmort.com, www.nrmla.org, or www.ffsenior.com. The first three cover the FHA home-equity conversion mortgage (HECM) and Fanny Mae's Home Keeper (HK) mortgage. The last one covers those plus the Financial Freedom cash account (CA) mortgage, which caters to high-priced homes (over $500,000). Based on the results, decide whether you want a reverse mortgage now, and, if so, which of the three types.

2. *Decide why you may want a reverse mortgage.* Why do you want a reverse mortgage? Because you have trouble paying the big bills that arrive, like property taxes? Because your lifestyle is crimped; even though you have a valuable house, you have trouble paying all your bills although you carefully limit how often you dine out and delay having your car checked? And it's a very old car. The best reason may be that you are, as the saying goes, house-rich and cash-poor.

If it is because you have one big bill that is overwhelming you, such as for a new roof, a home-equity loan might be better, or a loan from your community. A reverse mortgage is for people with a continual need for more income. If you are fairly sure why you want a reverse mortgage, you can more readily decide which kind of mortgage payment is best for you.

3. *Consider the alternatives.* Reread Chapter 4—on whether you should get a home-equity loan instead, whether you can sell your house to your children, and so forth.

4. *Write down any questions you may have.* Dumb questions are okay. Once you get your answer, you will know more than all those other people who are too embarrassed to ask that dumb question. Besides, at our age, people expect us to ask dumb questions. (A highlight of my long journalistic career came when I asked the director of the National Heart and Lung Institute in Washington, D.C., what the difference was between high blood pressure and hypertension. There was, he told me, no difference. Later I thought: My only mistake had been telling him which medical magazine an ignoramus like me worked for.)

5. *Find a reverse mortgage counselor and make an appointment.* See Chapter 7 for advice on choosing a counselor.

6. *Get counseled.* Counseling by a HUD-approved counseling agency is mandatory, regardless of what kind of loan you select, so use it as part of your education. You can find a counselor on your own by going to www.hud.gov/offices/hsg/sfh/hcc/hccprof14.cfm, clicking on your state, and selecting from among the agencies that list "HECM counseling."

You can also find a counselor through AARP. When you order its free consumer guide, AARP sends you information on its counseling referral system. AARP encourages you to read the booklet before you request counseling. Visit a counselor, ask questions, and obtain a certificate showing you were counseled.

7. *Decide on what kind of reverse mortgage you want.* Reread Chapters 9, 10, and 11. You will probably wind up with a HECM.

8. *Decide how you will get the funds.* For most people, a credit line plus a monthly income makes sense.

9. *If you get a HECM or Home Keeper, decide whether you want a monthly adjustable or yearly adjustable mortgage.* Most people choose the monthly adjustable.

10. *Select a lender who belongs to the National Reverse Mortgage Lenders Association (NRMLA).* These lenders subscribe to a code of conduct that prohibits deceptive or sharp practices. The code, as well as a list of members by state, is available on NRMLA's Web site (www.reversemortgage.org). Next to each NRMLA member's name is a notation of the types of loans the lender makes. All do HECMs. Most do HECMs and Home Keepers. A smaller number do cash accounts.

The lender will tell you the estimated cost of the loan and will ask for money for the appraisal.

The homeowner provides photo identification, evidence of his or her Social Security number, a copy of the deed to the home, information on any mortgages on the property, and the counseling certificate.

11. *Appraisal time.* If any repairs are needed, the homeowner must complete them before the mortgage closes.

12. *The closing, where the reverse-mortgage contract is signed.*

13. *The borrower begins receiving his or her money, or line of credit, and receives regular statements from the lender about the loan balance.*

14. *Eventually, the borrower or the borrower's estate repays the loan.*

14

Bringing Down Those High Closing Costs

As we saw in Chapter 2, John Butler of Ridgewood, New Jersey, saved a few thousand dollars by checking with several lenders before applying for a reverse mortgage. He saved on the "origination" fee, which is usually the key expense that patient borrowers can bring down. It can be as high as 2 percent of the lending limit ($6,257) set by the government. Another place you might save is on the monthly service fee, which can be as high as $35 a month.

Many lenders post estimates of their closing costs on their Internet sites.

How many lenders should you consult? A minimum of three, a number that comes from numerous experiments that tested how much money shoppers can save by shopping around. (See Exhibit 14.1.)

Originators must give you an estimate of the total cost of your obtaining a reverse mortgage—the total annual loan cost (TALC). This makes comparisons easier.

The National Center for Home Equity Conversion Web site (www.reverse.org), among others, has a calculator that estimates

Exhibit 14.1 Reverse Mortgage Comparison Worksheet

Loan Features	Lender 1	Lender 2	Lender 3
Lump sum option amount			
Line of credit option amount			
Monthly payment option amount			
Annual percentage rate (APR)			
Application fee			
Closing costs			
Other charges			

reverse-mortgage loan payments with different types of programs. The calculator also estimates the total annual loan cost (TALC) of a reverse mortgage, which includes both interest rates and fees. Your knowing a loan's TALC makes it easier for you to compare reverse mortgages offered by various lenders.

But it is only an estimate; no one knows for sure (1) whether the value of the house will go up or down while you live there and (2) how long you will live there. If you choose a line of credit, figuring out the cost will be even more complicated. How much will you borrow and when? And no one knows in advance what interest rate you will pay on the loan. Remember, it is an adjustable-rate loan.

Keep abreast of current interest rates. For local rates on mortgages, go to www.hsh.com or www.bankrate.com. Also, don't hesitate to lock in a good interest rate, Don't gamble with a short lock-in period.

While you are at it, see if the lender will agree (in writing) that if the closing costs are much more than the figures in the good-faith estimate, the lender will pay you the difference. "Much more" might be $500 or more.

Also, if you decide against a reverse mortgage, ask for all your papers back just to protect yourself against identity theft.

The Highest Cost

If you repay the loan within a few years, the cost will be highest. The up-front costs won't be spread out over a period of years. So, the longer you live in your home, the less expensive the loan will turn out to have been. (This is why I keep harping on your planning to remain in the home for three to five years.)

Surprisingly, if your home's value declines, the less expensive your loan will be. Why? Because the cost of your loan—the principal plus interest—is not allowed to surpass the value of your house. So, if your home's value when sold is $200,000, that's the amount that you will owe on the reverse mortgage. If your home's value had been $250,000, you could have owed $250,000.

But the bottom line is that you want your home to appreciate like mad. You hope that there will be a lot of value left even after you pay off the reverse mortgage. Instead of $250,000, you want your home to be worth $300,000—or a few million.

Appraisals

Homeowners refinancing their mortgages or obtaining home-equity loans are usually warned against "appraisal inflation." An appraisal on the high side may prompt them to borrow too much money, only to discover that their house wasn't worth as much as they had hoped. But with a reverse mortgage, a homeowner should not mind if an appraisal is somewhat over the top. He or she gets access to more money; the lender takes the risk if the house sells for less than its appraised value.

Your lender will hire an appraiser, and the cost to you may be $350 to $600. If you are not happy with the estimate, you can hire your own appraiser, although your lender may not accept any new figure. To find an appraiser, go to www.appraisalinstitute.org or www.naifa.com.

In 40 or so states, the government regulates title insurance premiums. In the others, you can shop around for the best rate on an owner's policy. Look for local companies at www.alta.org/search/state/cfm, which is sponsored by the American Land Title Association.

Homeowner's Insurance

With regard to homeowner's insurance, check the going rates every year, before your own policy ends. Get names of insurers from the Insurance Information Institute at www.iii.org. A few phone calls might save you several hundred dollars. If you are using an agent, don't assume that he or she is getting you the best rate.

One of the most respected insurers is USAA, open to army veterans and their families.

15

What to Do with All That Money

With your money, you have (1) things you must pay for, (2) things you probably should pay for, and (3) things you should consider paying for.

Things You Must Pay For

First of all, you must pay off your existing mortgage, if you have one. Also, you must pay the appraiser's bill and whatever other expenses cannot be folded into the loan itself. And you must pay to have your house repaired, fixing whatever an inspector reported was wrong with your place. Keep in mind that some contractors figure you will never ask anyone else for a bid, so they give you an outrageously high estimate.

Other necessary expenses: home insurance and property taxes. (Check with your municipality concerning whether people of your age are entitled to a tax break.) You can and probably should have these bills paid automatically by the bank, although that will lower your available cash; banks set aside the money in advance.

When looking for a repairperson, get bids if the work is extensive—maybe $500 or more. The Golden Rule is: Whenever a good deal of money is at stake, get three estimates. After three, the possible savings you may come away with tend to be small. (See Exhibit 15.1.)

Consider choosing the estimate in the middle. The lowest estimate may have come from someone desperate for work, someone willing to cut corners—to use lower-quality materials, for instance.

If one of the contractors enjoys a fine reputation and you want to wind up hiring that person, tell him or her what the other estimates were, and try to bargain the price down.

You can obtain names from your local hardware store, newspaper ads, or phone books. If there's a lot of work to do, test the first repairperson by giving him or her just one task. Was the charge reasonable; was the work done well and promptly? Did the worker clean up afterwards?

Usually it's better to pay people by the hour than by the project. If it's by the project, they may rush through it.

Regular maintenance of your house is a must. Either do it yourself, if you are able, or hire someone. Your lawn should be mowed regularly,

Exhibit 15.1 The Cost of Comfort

The cost of major improvements to make a home more suitable for older people can be high. The following estimates come from Legal Eagle Contractors in Houston, Texas. (Prices will be higher on the East and West Coasts.)

Adding an elevator: $30,000–$50,000 inside, $25,000–$30,000 outside.

Building an addition: $90,000–$175,000; average, $130,000.

Changing a bathtub to an accessible shower: $5,000–$6,000.

Installing a temperature- and pressure-balanced water valve (one that will not scald): $350–$500, plus $375 for a plumber.

Widening a door from 24 inches to 32 or 36: $750–$1,000.

Installing a stair glide on a staircase (to carry someone up and down stairs): $5,000.

Source: BusinessWeek, July 25, 2005.

and any problems, like dead patches, quickly remedied. Have your gutters regularly cleaned of leaves and debris; backed-up water can damage the roof. Walk through your house occasionally, looking for problems like a leaking roof, broken windows, or a nonworking heater. Remember: If you fail to maintain your house properly, the lender may insist that the loan is due. Uncut grass and broken windows are telltale signs.

Also, pay off any credit card bills you have because of their high interest rates. If you have a tendency to forget to pay them beyond their due dates, pay them just after they arrive.

Finally, you need an emergency fund. If you have a line of credit, that's your emergency fund. You can get cash whenever you wish. But if you chose to receive a lump sum, or a monthly income, set aside some cash to cover the unexpected, which may not be covered by your insurance policies. For example:

- The IRS decides that you underpaid your taxes and that you also owe a penalty.
- A friend or relative gets in trouble with the law, and you feel obliged to lend that person some money.
- You have a sudden and enormous expense—your furnace gives out, or your car gasps its last gasp.
- A regular source of income dries up—you lose your part-time job, for instance.

Your emergency fund should be liquid. You can get cash without your taking a big hit, as you might if you sold stocks or bonds at a bad time. A money-market fund is perfect; almost as good are short-term certificates of deposit or a short-term corporate bond mutual fund. Three respectable families of funds to consider setting up a money market account with are Vanguard, Fidelity, and T. Rowe Price.

The size of the emergency fund depends on you and your particular situation. Choose whatever amount you believe would help lessen the damage done by an unexpected high expense.

Things You Probably Should Pay For

Second are expenses that you should seriously consider, but are perhaps not absolutely necessary.

Long-Term Health-Care Insurance

Although 67 percent of Americans say that the cost of long-term care is the greatest threat to their standard of living, only 37 percent have done any planning for coverage. This is so even though the majority of care—custodial and intermediate—is not covered by Medicare.

Deena Katz, a CFP in Florida, has divided insurance into products that are (1) necessary and (2) not necessarily necessary. Among the first: health, automobile, and homeowners. Among the second: disability, life, and long-term care (in that order).

Her advice regarding long-term care insurance: if your assets (including your house) are worth $200,000 or less, you cannot afford it. Depend on Medicaid if you need long-term care.

Long-term care insurance can be frightfully expensive, and various authorities suggest that older people not buy the high-priced spread but buy the minimum. Salespeople, of course, may push the product with the most bells, whistles, and commissions.

A skeptical view comes from lawyer Joseph L. Matthews, author of *Long-Term Care: How to Plan & Pay for It* (Santa Cruz, CA: Nolo Press, fifth edition, 2004). He reports that authorities "generally agree that long-term care insurance is a bad investment—unless you can pay the monthly premium with no more than 5% of your income." And bear in mind, he adds, that those premiums will probably be rising while your income is dropping. As it is, 5 percent is a no small percentage: It is $3,000 of $60,000.

His solution is very risky. Even if you expect to be well-to-do in your old age, he writes, "A financial advisor may show you more profitable ways of investing the same money you would put into insurance premiums. And those investments plus permissible transfers of assets under Medicaid rules may combine to provide better protection and liquidity for your money than a long-term care insurance policy."

Yet he gives these worthwhile suggestions about choosing a policy:

- Check several policies for their exclusions and limitations. Look for policies "covering the broadest types of care that might be useful to you," like home care, custodial care, and assisted-living residences.
- Avoid any policy that requires a stay in a hospital or skilled-nursing facility before it covers long-term care.

- Avoid a policy that permanently excludes any conditions, such as mental illness, alcohol or chemical dependency, diabetes, certain forms of cancer, and HIV-related illnesses.
- Ignore mail-order or limited-time-only policies.
- Don't buy "any policy touted in an advertisement that uses an exclamation point."
- Don't be guided in your decision by a single insurance agent or broker. Insurance agents, Matthews writes, "are in the business of selling policies—not of warning you why you should not buy one. Although most agents are conscientious about not selling a policy they know is not right for a customer, some will say almost anything to make a sale."

An attractive idea is to ask your children to pay for your policy. After all, such a policy can help ensure that someday they will have assets to inherit.

Financial planners have told me that the two most reliable companies providing long-term health-care insurance are General Electric and John Hancock.

Life Insurance

For most seniors life insurance is a dubious buy, even though you see ads for such insurance on Web sites about reverse mortgages. Several other forms of insurance also belong on a do-not-buy list. (See the next chapter.)

Occasionally life insurance is appropriate for estate planning purposes. Here is an example given by Wells Fargo in a press release.

A 75-year-old widow has an annual income of $75,000 from a $1 million municipal-bond portfolio and her late husband's $500,000 IRA. With the $75,000, she can live comfortably in her home of 23 years.

But she wants to give a good deal of money to her children. So, following the advice of her financial adviser, she buys a life insurance policy. But how can she pay the premiums without selling some of her assets, thus reducing her income?

The solution: a reverse mortgage. Her home was worth $750,000, and she qualified for a $218,875 loan. With the $218,875, she bought a single-premium immediate annuity, with an after-tax payment of $20,000 every year. This $20,000 payment was directed into a trust, which bought a $600,000 life insurance policy for her heirs.

Her reverse mortgage, by in effect shrinking her equity in her house, reduced the taxable portion of her estate. The life insurance policy increased the nontaxable portion. Combined, this boosted her estate's after-tax value by as much as 32 percent. So her heirs could inherit much more, while her own income was not affected, and she could live in her house as long as she wished.

Of course, the financial adviser didn't do badly, either, with commissions on the annuity and the life insurance policy.

Income Annuities

As for annuities, which are a form of insurance, an income (immediate) annuity is a distinct possibility. (See Chapter 5.) A deferred annuity is probably not. (See Chapter 16.)

Financial Planners

A reverse mortgage counselor can help you with your finances, but is no substitute for a financial planner—someone who will look over your entire financial picture, including your insurance, your investments, your will, your tax forms, and your spending. This almost qualifies as a necessity. As mentioned in Chapter 7, Type 1 borrowers, those who need money as opposed to wanting it, could hire planners who charge by the hour and thus not get hit with staggering bills. Other professional advisers to call upon are, of course, tax advisers and lawyers.

Modifying Your House

A true tale of terror: Lizbeth Chapman, 57, moved from Boston to a house in Wellfleet, Massachusetts, intending to spend the remainder of her life there. Then she broke her ankle and ended up in a cast that prevented her from walking. "I was virtually immobile for three months," she said. Confined to a wheelchair, "The house became a prison."

Her solution may have been a bit drastic. She had her 55-year-old cottage torn down and a new home constructed—one more suitable for older people, for people who want to "age in place." (*BusinessWeek* July 25, 2005.)

A sensible way for people with reverse mortgages to use their new-found money is to make their houses safer and more comfortable, assuming that the cost would not be extravagant.

Most home improvements do not pay for themselves. When you sell your home, you will be lucky to get back 75 percent of your improvement money. By upgrading a bathroom or kitchen, you are most likely to come out even. And, fortunately, the bathroom and kitchen are the prime targets for older people seeking more safety and comfort.

For only a few thousand dollars, you can make a house safer and more comfortable for an older person, Bill Asdal of Chester, New Jersey, maintains. Asdal, a remodeler, mentions such low-cost changes as:

- Substituting door latches for round doorknobs— easier for everyone.
- Switching from double-hung windows (one window over the other) to casement windows, which open and close with cranks (so, for example, you don't have to lean over a sink to open or close a window).
- Installing a door with the hinges set inside the door, so the door can open further (the extra two inches helps accommodate wheelchairs and walkers).
- Installing 3-inch, D-shaped drawer pulls, which are easier to use.
- Putting grab bars in the shower and bathroom.
- Removing the floor sills from all rooms, to prevent tripping.

Some of these changes are so simple you can do them yourself or hire a local handyperson.

For older people, the "most troublesome" part of a house is the bathroom, followed by the kitchen, according to Reza Ahmadi. He and Kay Hodson Carlton are directors of the WellCome Home Project and professors at Ball State University in Muncie, Indiana. Bathrooms are used constantly, Ahmadi notes, while people can give up cooking in their kitchens. And bathrooms tend to be tiny: 5 feet by 7 feet.

Older people might convert one of their rooms into a study—a spare bedroom, for instance. They will be spending more time at home than they did during their working days. A downstairs bathroom would also be a good idea. Also, if the homeowners extend the paving on their lawn, they will have less gardening work to do.

But at this point, when the cost may be high, you should consider moving. This is particularly the case with smaller, older houses, in which space to expand may be wanting.

In dealing with remodelers, make sure that your contract has a detailed description of what work will be done, including the date the project will be completed, the materials to be used, the cost, and any guarantees. Try not to add anything after the project has begun. That can cause the cost to skyrocket.

Get at least three bids. Then return to the remodeler with the best reputation, and try to get that remodeler—if his or her bid was high—to meet or beat the lowest bid.

One of the worst mistakes you can make is hiring someone who comes cheap because he or she is trying to break into the business. All of us sympathize with beginners, but recall the immortal words of Roy Neuberger, the money manager: "I don't want a barber to learn how to shave by practicing on my face." My own parents once hired an inexperienced builder to build them a new house. A nightmare. I recall getting out of bed one morning, after sleeping in the basement, and stepping into two feet of cold water.

Signs of beginners: They drive an unmarked truck or a truck with out-of-state plates. They have only a cell phone. no established office. They cannot provide references, or only a few who may be their relatives or friends. And they demand cash up front.

Making houses more accessible to older people. or for the disabled in general, is the newest thing in remodeling. Today, there are even local remodelers designated as Certified Aging in Place Specialists by the National Association of the Remodeling Industry (NARI).

Builders in general are also being encouraged to pursue "universal design" so that the houses they construct are safe and comfortable not just for the young and healthy but for the elderly and ill. As Asdal notes, houses usually have been single-family stand-alones, built for healthy young and middle-aged people, not for the elderly and the infirm.

But with the aging of the population, houses built for the old as well as for the young are clearly needed. "Universal design isn't the highest on our list of requests by homeowners, but it's on the rise," said Joan Stephens of Boise, Ohio, former president of NARI.

How costly a modification is depends to a large degree on how extensive the changes will be. "If you must move a wall or make corridors wider for wheelchairs with a five-foot radius wheelbase, expect high costs," Ahmadi warns.

The average cost of aging-in-place remodelings in general, he estimates, may be between $5,000 and $7,000.

One handicap that remodelers have is that the elderly don't want their houses to look "institutional," like a hospital. So, whenever possible, changes must be subtle and harmonious.

NARI has proposed seven basic principles that incorporate universal design for homeowners who are thinking of remodeling:

1. The design should suit any type of user, not just the elderly but the young as well.
2. The design should be usable by people with a wide range of abilities— the unskilled and the skilled.
3. The design should be easy to understand.
4. Information about the design should be easy to find.
5. The design should minimize the danger of accidents.
6. The design should make hard work not necessary.
7. The area should be the right size.

To find a remodeler, go online to www.Remodeltoday.com for a member of NARI, or call 800- 611-NARI. Members must adhere to a code of ethics or risk being drummed out of the organization.

A fine Web site, www.bsu.edu/WELLcomeHome, developed by Ahmadi and Carlton, includes a test to determine how accessible a house is for older people, a quiz, and a detailed description of desired changes. (See appendices 1 and 2.)

Ahmadi and Carlton make these eloquent points on their Web site:

- "The home is a power base in social interaction, a fount of personal meaning and biography, a familiar and therefore navigable environment, and, not least, a financial cushion."
- Older people in particular tend to live in older homes that need repairs or modifications. Over 60 percent live in homes more than 20 years old.

- One-third to one-half of home accidents can be prevented by modification and repairs.
- "For many older people, there is a virtual equivalence between health and home."

For suggestions on home modifications, see Appendix 1.

Things You Should Consider Paying For

This third, final category is for uses of money that are not essential and, perhaps, not even desirable for all borrowers. Uses might include investing and bestowing gifts. They are more appropriate for Type 2 borrowers, those who, unlike Type 1 borrowers, don't *need* extra money; they just *want* it.

Investing

Should anyone with a reverse mortgage invest in anything at all? The argument has been made that it's unwise. These people are borrowing money at, say, 5 percent, so their investments must earn more than that 5 percent. And if interest rates rise, that 5 percent bogey will climb, too, because theirs is an adjustable-rate mortgage.

This is what AARP advises: "Investing the money you get from a reverse mortgage is a highly questionable practice. It is extremely unlikely that you could safely earn more from an investment than the loan would cost."

The argument against investing reverse-mortgage money certainly carries weight with borrowers who have little margin for error—Type 1 borrowers. If you can barely pay your bills, it is not the right time to try making a killing in the stock market. This is especially true considering that so many people who obtain reverse mortgages are widows, many of whom have little or no investment knowledge or experience.

Besides which, ordinary investors tend to make the same costly mistakes again and again. They buy top-performing stocks just when they are vastly overpriced; when these stocks fall, and perhaps become reasonably priced, investors—depressed, despairing—sell out. One of the few eternal verities about the stock market is that the average investor will buy high and sell low.

Still another strike against the ordinary investor: he or she may not know the fundamental rules, such as that you need at least 15 or 20 stocks in different industries to have a decently diversified portfolio, one that is unlikely to blow up on you.

Compounding the fact that many seniors are babes in the woods when it comes to investing, the investment world itself, especially the stock market, is fraught with danger. Stocks can go down and remain down for a long time. From 1929 through 1932, the stock market lost 80 percent of its value. If you had invested in stocks in 1929, you would not have been made whole until the late 1930s. Another terrible bear market occurred in 1972–1973, when the stock market lost 48 percent of its value. Then there was the Tech Wreck of 2000, when small-company stocks lost 50 percent of their value, and large-company stocks lost 20 percent of theirs.

Considering how treacherous the stock market is, why do so many people load up on stocks?

- If you own a diversified portfolio of stocks, one that has exposure to a variety of industries, and you hold on through thick and thin, you will probably do very well. Over the years, stocks have climbed some 11 percent a year, and the profits usually have been taxed leniently.
- Investing in stocks is fun. It is like gambling, only the odds against you are not as high, especially if you diversify.
- A good many money managers recommend that everyone should have a huge exposure to stocks, the usual argument being that if you retire at 65, you will probably live into your 80s, and you may need the protection against inflation that stocks may provide. But these days treasury inflation protected securities (TIPS) can accomplish that. And if you keep a huge percentage of your portfolio in stocks when you are age 65 and the market goes into one of its usual tailspins, you will be in big trouble. People who retired in 1973, just when a bear market began, and who had a sizable exposure to the stock market ran out of money fairly quickly.

As persuasive as the avoid-stocks case is, there is also a good case for buying stocks. This advice comes from the Bank of New York: "A reverse mortgage could also be used to fund investments. Since the interest rate is equal to the One-Year Treasury bill plus a 1.5 percent margin, there is a possibility that the reverse mortgage proceeds, properly invested, would outgain the accruing interest."

It is a tough problem, and the answer may be that Type 1 borrowers should by and large avoid investing, whereas Type 2 borrowers should invest carefully, with much depending upon how sophisticated and skillful they and their advisers are and how they would be able to cope in a prolonged bear market.

For Type 2 borrowers, putting some money—not necessarily reverse-mortgage money—into different investments would help diversify their assets, which would be especially appropriate if almost all their wealth is in their house. House prices can go down nationally, if (for example) interest rates rise and first-time homebuyers can no longer afford mortgages, and locally, if (for example) a large employer in the area moves out. For the house-very-rich, keeping some reverse-mortgage money in securities is probably wise, perhaps 20 to 40 percent of their investment portfolios, with the remainder in fixed-income investments like CDs and tax-exempt bonds. (See Exhibit 15.2.)

Exhibit 15.2 Taxable vs. Tax-Exempt Bonds

Many people are reluctant to invest in tax-free municipal bonds because they are afraid of getting into trouble with Uncle Sam. Other people invest in munis even though they would be better off in taxables.

Munis pay less than taxables, but the higher your "marginal tax bracket," the more you should buy munis. (A marginal tax bracket is the highest percentage that your income is taxed.) But keep in mind that certain munis are subject to the alternative minimum tax.

To calculate whether taxables or tax-exempt bonds are right for you, subject your tax rate (say, 28 percent) from 1. So, $1 - 0.28 = 0.72$.

Divide the result into the tax-free yield (say, 0.5 percent): $0.5/0.72 = 6.94$.

So, the tax-free yield is equal to a taxable yield of 6.94 percent. A taxable bond, in this case, would have to yield 6.94 percent to equal a 5 percent tax-free yield.

For conservative investors, mutual funds and not individual stocks are the safer course. With a mutual fund, you usually get a well-diversified portfolio, often with an experienced and skillful money manager, whose investment philosophy you can study and whose track record you can check. (However, a strong case can be made for buying low-cost index funds, which simply buy a sampling of an investment market. This would enable the purchaser to dispense with a money manager.)

Morningstar Mutual Funds, a newsletter published in Chicago, rates mutual funds from one star to five stars (best), based on their performances versus their peers, and even recommends particular funds. (A high-rated fund may not be worth buying if the manager just left.) Even more useful, a sister publication, *Morningstar FundInvestor,* regularly publishes entire portfolios of mutual funds, including one specifically for retirees. Call Morningstar at 866-608-9570 to ask for a sample copy.

For older people, income funds are probably the best choice. These are funds that buy bonds and dividend-paying stocks. They are a fairly conservative investment for people who have a yellow streak down their spines (like me), who are fearful of losing a lot of money should stocks behave as shamefully as they did during the bear markets of 1973–1974 and 1929–1932. Even so, despite their being diversified, despite their buying safer stocks, and despite their owning conservative bonds, they are risky. All investments in the stock market are risky.

An income fund is like an immediate or income annuity, only better because it may continue to grow as long as you live (if you don't sell), and you can bequeath it to your heirs. But, unlike an income annuity, an income fund guarantees nothing. You could wind up losing most of your money.

There are, unfortunately, big differences among funds that call themselves income funds.

PIMCO Diversified Income recently had nothing in stocks; T. Rowe Price Personal Strategy Income had 46 percent. (More than 46 percent, and you may have a "balanced" fund.) Vanguard Wellesley Income recently had 37.6 percent in stocks; Vanguard Target Retirement Income, a mere 20 percent.

Morningstar no longer has a category for income funds; the closest thing it has these days is "conservative allocation."

The typical fund in this category, according to Morningstar, has 34.9 percent in stocks (15.4 percent foreign); 44 percent in bonds; 14 percent in cash; and 7.1 percent in "other."

The stocks these funds own are mostly giant and large, and they seem not very different from stocks in the Standard & Poor's 500, apart from being more reasonably priced in general. Stocks that are overrepresented in such portfolios include: Merck, Pfizer, Bank of America, Ameren, and Dominion Resources. The bonds are high-rated (AA), with an average effective maturity of 6.4 years.

One of the oldest income funds is Vanguard Wellesley Income, which was launched in 1970.

Stocks, as mentioned, make up 37.6 percent of Vanguard's portfolio; bonds, 60.3 percent. Cash makes up 1.9 percent, and 0.2 percent is in other investments. The portfolio is tilted toward giant and large value stocks, such as ExxonMobil, Bank of America, and Citigroup. The yearly turnover (how much trading went on) in 2004 was only 23 percent. The recent yield was a pleasing 3.9 percent. All Vanguard funds have low expenses.

The fund gets a five-star rating from Morningstar. Its most recent down year came in 1999, when it dropped by 4.14 percent.

Although the fund's effective maturity is 7.7 percent, Morningstar warns that the "portfolio's sensitivity to interest-rate fluctuations can't be ignored." (The main enemy of bonds is a rise in interest rates, and the longer the maturity, the more vulnerable a bond is.) Even so, it's a Morningstar "analyst pick." To obtain information, call 800-662-7447. The minimum first investment is $3,000.

Another Vanguard income fund worth considering is Vanguard Target Retirement Income, launched in 2003. A fund of index funds, it has only 20 percent in stocks; 74 percent is in bonds, including 25 percent in Treasury Inflation Protected Securities. And 5.9 percent is in cash. This is much safer than Wellesley Income.

Also more conservative than Wellesley Income is T. Rowe Price Spectrum Income, which Morningstar lists as a "multi-sector bond fund." But this fund recently had 16.4 percent in stocks; the average multisector bond fund, including Spectrum Income, had a mere 1.7 percent in stocks.

Spectrum Income is composed of various T. Rowe Price funds, mostly bond funds, such as high yield and Ginnie Mae, but also including a stock fund: Equity-Income. Besides those stocks, the fund has 58.7 percent in bonds, 9.6 percent in cash, and 15.3 percent in "other" (including restricted securities). Recent yield: 4.1 percent. Average effective maturity: 6.6 years. Average credit quality: only B (because of those junk bonds).

As Morningstar notes, the fund gives investors an "incredibly broad exposure" to bonds, including a smidgeon of emerging-market debt. Its last losing year came in 1994, with a loss of only 1.93 percent. Spectrum Income is another "analyst pick." For information, call 800-638-5660. The minimum investment is $2,500.

Still another choice worth considering is Fidelity Asset Manager: Income. It's only 19 percent in stocks (14.9 percent of which is foreign), along with 39.1 percent in bonds, a huge 37.3 percent in cash, and 4.6 percent in "other." Recent yield: 2 percent. Its stocks, surprisingly, tend to be growth stocks: Microsoft, Nextel, DR Horton. The average stock's price-earnings ratio and price-book ratio are relatively high. Its last losing year: 2002, down only 0.5 percent. It returned 5.71 percent in 1999, which was a year that Wellesley Income lost money.

Morningstar suggests that Fidelity Freedom Fund may be an even better choice because it's a fund of funds. But that fund, too, has a huge amount in money markets. Even so, Morningstar rates Asset Manager: Income "above average." For information, call 800-343-3548. The minimum investment is $2,500.

I would prefer to buy an income fund from a big, prosperous family. Hence I have zeroed in on Vanguard, T. Rowe Price, and Fidelity.

Wellesley Income is the riskiest, with its relatively high exposure to stocks. It has returned 8.78 percent a year for five years. Fidelity Asset Manager: Income, with its huge stake in cash, may be the safest and has returned 5.08 percent a year; Spectrum Income, with its junk bonds, is in between and has returned 8.17 percent. If you can swing it, investing in a variety of income funds makes sense. I own shares of all three.

How much of a portfolio an older person should have in the stock market depends on the person's need for income, risk tolerance, and overall wealth (which means the ability to cope during an extended bear market). But 20 to 40 percent would probably be the consensus among financial advisers.

Gifts

If you have money to spare, a thoughtful gift would be a contribution to a grandchild's college savings plan. The money you contribute to a 529 Savings Plan grows untaxed if it is kept in an adult's name, with a child as the beneficiary, and if it's used for a college education. Even when withdrawn, the money is not taxed (though that might change).

A good 529 plan has low expenses, and its investments become more conservative as a child grows older, moving from stocks to bonds. All the states offer 529 plans, and one of the most admired is Michigan's plan, run by TIAA-CREF. Not admired is Rhode Island's plan and Arizona's SMR plan.

Anyone in any state can use an out-of-state plan. Still, if you get a tax deduction for contributing to a plan in your state, consider your state's plan. New Yorkers can deduct $10,000 for a couple filing jointly, $5,000 for an individual.

You can contribute as much as $305,000 to one account in some 529 plans in one year. For information about the various plans, go to www.savingforcollege.com.

Independent 529 plans are a little different. They are prepaid tuition plans: Money you put in will appreciate at the same rate as tuition at various private colleges. But at this point, only 250 colleges are taking part, and among the missing are Harvard, Yale, and Columbia.

16

What *Not* to Do with Your Money

A financial planner once told me that she had received a phone call from an excited client who had just won a lottery of about $30,000. "Don't do a thing until we get together," the planner told the woman. The client came in several days later, down in the dumps. All her newfound money was gone. Giving new cars as presents to your relatives is expensive.

Acquiring a large sum of money all at once can be intoxicating. You feel wonderful: You have finally proved to everyone, even skeptics, how worthy you are. You have finally ascended into heaven, where you belonged all along.

It is certainly one of the keenest pleasures in life, and many people feel it for the very first time when they sell their houses. I remember the very first time I was thrilled with the thought of how rich I was. I was a young man, it was 30 years ago, and I had sold my first house for $60,000.

The first thing to do with any bundle of money you receive—whether from the lottery, from the racetrack, from the sale of a book, or from a reverse mortgage—is *nothing*.

According to Marylou Reeves, CFP, of Rockaway, New Jersey, "The most common mistake is that people feel they have to invest the princely sum overnight. But investing all at once could be a disaster. Also, the money may be dissipated on luxuries and nonessentials. There are horror stories of people winning the lottery, yet having nothing after just a few years, and worse yet having destroyed relationships with friends and family because the lottery winner would not lend money to a family member, or, if the money was lent, it was never paid back.

"If you do come into a large sum, set aside 5 percent or some small amount that is just to be 'blown' away without guilt or justification, then commit yourself to investing the rest, either for yourself, your retirement, or your children's education."

And the first thing you might do is hire a financial planner to advise you. (See Chapter 7.)

Just be careful whom you ask help from. AARP, which is foursquare in favor of reverse mortgages, has warned that borrowers should "be cautious of anyone who seems eager for you to get a reverse mortgage. Be especially alert if that person just happens to have ideas about what you might do with the loan proceeds. Watch out in particular for anyone trying to sell you something, or to get your signature on an agreement to pay them for any purpose."

The second thing you might do is divide the money in your mind. What are your needs? What are your wants? How much do you need to pay your current debts, including your credit card bills? How much will you want to spend just to celebrate? How much will you sock away into a money market fund as an emergency fund?

Obviously, you should avoid risky investments or simply unusual ones—anything you don't really understand. The old advice still holds: if it seems too good to be true, it probably is. If you are not sure, check with one of your advisers—your financial planner, your lawyer, your accountant, or your financial counselor.

Following is a discussion of specific things you should be wary about buying.

Deferred Annuities

Deferred annuities are the most popular kind of annuity, yet they are ill-suited for many of the people who purchase them. A much better choice would be income annuities.

Robert D. Nestor, a principal at the Vanguard Group in Malverne, Pennsylvania, believes that deferred annuities are oversold because the salespeople make enormous commissions. Few if any other investment products, he points out, reward salespeople so handsomely.

Annuities are investments that are exempt from taxes while they grow, presumably to be used as retirement income.

"If they are the least suitable," Nestor asked about deferred annuities, "why are they the biggest?" Besides the commissions they pay, he gave these reasons:

- They look like mutual funds, which people are familiar with.
- They help people avoid taxes (although people should be more concerned with their after-tax returns).
- The financial penalties for early withdrawal persuade investors to stick with them.

"Income annuities are much more suitable," Nestor said, "but they are the least-understood kind of annuity." He explained that there are basically two kinds of annuities:

1. *Deferred,* in which you are expected to withdraw the money sometime in the future.
2. *Income* or immediate annuities, in which you give an insurance company a lump sum, and in a month or so you start receiving money to live on for the rest of your life.

Both kinds of annuities are further divided into either "variable annuities," which may invest in stocks and bonds, and "fixed annuities," which may invest in a bond.

A variable annuity may be suitable for people seeking tax-deferred growth of their assets for retirement, because of the stocks it can invest in. But the costs are high—2.25 percent a year on average compared with 1.25 percent for the average mutual fund. "Most investors would be better off in mutual funds," Nestor said. On the other hand, a deferred fixed annuity can be "very appropriate for a conservative investor." Even so, he cautioned: "Read the fine print." Beware of a high early-withdrawal penalty, called a *surrender charge,* that may last seven years or longer.

As for when to buy an income annuity, Nestor recommended that people wait until they are in their late 60s or early 70s and limit their purchases to 25 percent of their assets. He also recommended buying income annuities at different times, in case interest rates rise quickly.

For a copy of Vanguard's booklet "Should You Consider an Income Annuity," phone Vanguard at 800-662-7447 or visit Vanguard.com and print out the booklet.

Revocable Living Trusts

Most older people without sizable assets don't need a "revocable living trust," which lets you put your assets into a trust and control them during your lifetime. When you die, the assets in the trust go directly to your heirs, bypassing the costs and delays of probate court. (A probate court makes sure that the provisions of a will are carried out.) But you don't need a living trust unless you have a large, varied estate, you live in a state that requires probate, or there are other special problems.

Consumer Reports MoneyAdviser (May 2004) reports that 34 states have simplified their probate procedures: Alabama, Alaska, Arizona, Arkansas, California, Colorado, Florida, Georgia, Hawaii, Idaho, Illinois, Indiana, Iowa, Louisiana, Maine, Massachusetts, Michigan, Minnesota, Missouri, Montana, Nebraska, New Jersey, New Mexico, New York, North Dakota, Pennsylvania, Rhode Island, South Dakota, Tennessee, Texas, Utah, Washington, West Virginia, and Wisconsin.

Life Insurance

If you have complicated estate problems, a life-insurance policy may be appropriate, as is mentioned in Chapter 15. But for most people, that is not the case. Plus, federal estate taxes are heading downward. (See Exhibit 16.1.)

Life insurance may be appropriate for extremely wealthy people, to cover their estate taxes after they die. But estate taxes are slated to dimin-

Exhibit 16.1 The Federal Estate Tax Is Losing Its Bite

Year	Exemption Amount	Maximum Federal Tax Rate
2006	$2 million	46 percent
2007–2008	$2 million	45 percent
2009	$3.5 million	45 percent
2010	Repeal of estate tax	
2011	Returns to $1 million	55 percent

Note: The amount exempt from the estate tax is reduced by the gift-tax exemption amount someone used over a lifetime for gifts to individuals above the annual gift-tax exclusion amount.

ish in the years ahead, so life insurance in general remains questionable for older people.

"Generally, the purchase of life insurance in your later years is not recommended," advises Patricia Q. Brennan, CFP, a tenured professor at Rutgers University in New Jersey. "It is a very costly proposition, and your premium dollars can usually be better spent."

"Life insurance makes sense," she goes on, "if you have dependents who would suffer financially if you died. But carry too much and you may not enjoy a reasonable level of living.

"Once your children are grown and you've accumulated assets over several decades, your need for life insurance coverage should decrease.

"Rather than your adding life insurance at this time, save those premium dollars to fund some of the goals of life insurance, such as covering financial expenses, reducing outstanding debt, or buying long-term health-care insurance."

Unfortunately, as Graydon Calder, CFP, CLU, of San Diego, California, once said, insurance agents think that insurance is the solution to all of humanity's problems—including a clogged-up kitchen sink.

One Web site gives useful information about reverse mortgages and then urges borrowers to obtain life insurance. "By purchasing a life insurance policy for your heirs with funds from a reverse mortgage," reads the site, "you know exactly what you are leaving behind." Not a very sensible argument. You would probably leave a lot more behind if you put those premiums into a stock mutual fund. Besides which, if someone dies soon after obtaining a reverse mortgage, that person will not have used up much of the equity in the house. His or her heirs should inherit a significant amount without insurance.

Other Forms of Insurance

It's interesting that there are so many forms of insurance that people should avoid. Is it because the word "insurance" is so reassuring? Is it because insurance salespeople have trouble selling life insurance (because people don't want to think about their mortality), so they turn to other forms?

Whatever the answer, here are 10 more insurance policies you don't need, even if you are still working, according to *Consumer Reports* (July 2004):

1. *Mortgage life insurance.* To pay off your mortgage if you die. Buy term life instead—plain vanilla insurance, without a savings account.
2. *Credit card loss protection.* Federal law limits your loss to $50 a card.
3. *Car-rental insurance.* Your own auto policy should provide such coverage.
4. *Flight insurance.* Your term insurance will cover you if you die in a plane crash, and your health insurance should cover any medical expenses.
5. *Cancer insurance.* Your existing health insurance policy probably covers it.
6. *Credit life insurance.* Covers your debts if you die. Term life would do.
7. *Credit disability insurance.* Will pay installments on a loan, typically up to 36 months, if you are disabled. Just be sure that if you have a disability plan, it will cover your expenses, including any loan payments.
8. *Involuntary unemployment insurance.* This policy makes minimum payments on loans for 6 to 12 months if you lose your job. Just have an emergency fund instead.

9. *Accidental-death insurance.* Hardly anyone dies in an accident. Stick with term life insurance.
10. *Identity theft insurance.* Instead, just check your credit reports regularly.

Fraudulent Investments

Remember: the more successful the con artist, the bigger the lies he or she tells. You and I may feel: "No one could tell a lie like that with a straight face." Such as: "Double your money in six months!" But people would and do. An intelligent woman I know, a nurse, told me that someone sold her some mutual funds and assured her that the salespeople didn't charge her a penny. She told me the names of the funds. They were load funds, funds that carry commissions.

"Why do you think they didn't charge you?" I asked her.

A pause. "They liked me?"

For more on fraud, see Chapter 17.

17

Time to Repay the Loan

The owners (or their heirs) don't have to repay the loan immediately after the last owner no longer lives in the house. They have a full year—or more, if they submit a letter of intent explaining any delay. For example, there may be a court battle among the heirs over what to do with the house. Or the house may simply need more repairs.

The loan ends when

- The last borrower moves out of the house permanently—for 12 consecutive months.
- The last borrower dies.
- A new owner is added.
- The borrower does not pay the property taxes or home insurance or lets the house fall into disrepair. (Normal wear and tear is acceptable.)
- The owners sell the house.
- Part of the house is rented.

The company servicing the loan will probably check with you once a year to see that you are still living in the house, either by phone or by letter with a preaddressed return form. If the servicer cannot reach you, the servicer will probably communicate with the alternative person you listed in the contract, possibly a relative, friend, or lawyer whom you named.

In any case, you should inform the lender that you have moved out of the house, and you should let your heirs know that they are responsible for handling this if you cannot do it yourself.

In most cases, the house winds up being sold. That is a simple, efficient way to repay the debt, and it has much to recommend it.

What you will owe is *not* the sum of the loan, the interest, and any closing-cost expenses that were financed. It will be that sum *minus* the net sales price of the house. Your debt is limited by the value of the house. Neither you nor your heirs can owe a penny more.

In most cases, thanks to the appreciation of the house and property, there should be some money left over.

How Much Will You Owe?

The lender will let you know what you owe. But expect to owe more if any of the following applies:

- You took out a lump sum. In that case, the meter began ticking immediately. If you took out a line of credit, it's likely you will owe less than you would otherwise, especially if you seldom used that line of credit.
- You lived in the house a long time rather than a short time.
- You did not repay any of the loan beforehand.
- You borrowed the maximum amount you could borrow.
- Interest rates rose over the years rather than remaining stable or declining. (Reverse mortgages have adjustable rates, meaning that they go up when interest rates in general go up.)

You can estimate what you or your estate will owe by checking your total annual cost estimate (TALC), which your lender was required to give you when you first obtained the loan. Multiply that yearly estimated cost by the number of years you have actually lived in the house. But keep in mind that that estimate was only an estimate. The TALC guesses at how many years you will live in the house, guesses as to what sort of loan you took out, and guesses as to where interest rates will go.

The final bill itself will include the principal loan amount plus all the interest. If you did not pay them already, the tab will also include the origination fees, closing costs, and servicing fees—and the interest on them as well.

Should You Prepay?

Prepaying the loan is a smart move if you can afford it, especially if interest rates have just gone up and if you received a lump sum. Direct that the prepayment go toward the interest you owe, not the principal, so that you can tax-deduct the interest (if you can itemize on your return). Ask your lender how it prefers prepayments to be handled.

You may not be able to repay a loan if you received a monthly income, but you can repay a line of credit and a lump sum. Two of the Financial Freedom loans do not permit repayments for five years.

Repaying a reverse mortgage will in part lower the total interest you will eventually owe, along with reducing your total debt. And it may even allow you to borrow more in the future should you need to.

Bill Agner, director of reverse mortgages for the Mortgage Network in Indianapolis, makes a sensible suggestion: Don't pay off a reverse mortgage entirely because you may need another reverse mortgage soon, and the closing costs could be substantial. You might pay off most of the existing mortgage, but keep $1,000 in a line of credit so that the mortgage remains in effect.

If You Sell the House

In selling the house, naturally you or your heirs should try to come away with the largest amount you can obtain. After all, any money left over beyond the debt will belong to you or your heirs. (In case the house is sold after your demise, indicate in your will how any leftover money should be distributed.)

To save money, you might try selling the house yourself, without an agent. If you have sales experience and real estate experience, this can work. But for amateurs it can be dangerous: There are a good many crooks out there who prey on "fisbos" (people who try to sell their houses them-selves—For Sale By Owner). For example, they may agree to buy your house for $200,000. Then, on the day of the closing, they bring a check for $180,000. That is all they can afford, they coolly tell you. Take it or leave it. (This actually happened to a relative of mine. She walked out of the meeting.)

These sleazy buyers make it a practice of offering reasonable bids for houses and then at the last minute offering much less, counting on the sellers accepting because they are, at this point, almost desperate for the deal to go through. They may have a condo in Florida they have already purchased; a moving company may be coming next week. Then the buyers, having bought the house cheaply, will proceed to sell it for a swift and sizable profit.

The lesson to be learned here is that if you try to sell your house yourself, hire a real estate lawyer as soon as you can. A lawyer would have seen to it that the terms of the sale that had been agreed upon orally, including the sales price, had been put in writing. In real estate, oral promises are generally worthless.

Instead of trying to sell the house yourself, you might take an intermediate step by hiring a discount broker. Instead of charging 5 or 6 percent commission, the discount broker may charge 2 or 3 percent. But such brokers generally don't do all the work that traditional brokers do, such as actually showing the house to potential buyers. Still, if you are in no great rush and you are able to help out, you might try a discount broker for a short period of time. Don't be pressured into signing a contract for longer than three months. The longer the contract, the less hard any real estate agent may work.

When you hire a real estate agent, pay more attention to the agent than to the company. A good company is fine, but the agent comes first. Look for an agent who has special certifications, an agent who is serious about his or her career. You want someone who actually sells houses, not just lists them for other agents to sell. When you interview agents, ask them how many houses they have sold during the past year. But be warned that some agents are so intent on selling houses that they try to underprice them, so they go fast.

These days, agents may be willing to cut their commissions, to have a record proving that they don't always charge 6 or 7 percent.

If you are interviewing agents, inquire about their marketing strategy. Are they in touch with the human resources departments of local employers, so they know when newcomers are moving to town? In what media do they advertise? How do they manage to meet new people?

In most cases, discourage friends or relatives who want to list your house for sale. Tell them that years ago you promised you would list your house with so-and-so.

In preparing the house for sale, avoid certain common mistakes such as the ones that follow:

- Do fix things that need fixing. Buyers may become discouraged when they see a lot of work needs to be done and conclude that if you neglected small things, you must have neglected big things.
- Recognize that many buyers are unimaginative. If the wallpaper is faded but you lowered your asking price to cover the cost of new wallpaper, the buyers may prefer a house with new wallpaper, even for a little more money.
- Don't expect the buyers to have the same cultivated taste that you have. In redecorating, bland is the word. In fact, try to deal with anything especially unusual about your house, such as a darkroom. Say, for example, that the darkroom would make a good office.
- Before your house is shown, take down family photographs, awards you have won, and other distinctive signs emphasizing your ownership. They have a negative psychological effect on buyers.
- Be mindful that the first offer is often the best offer. But beware of "low balls"—outrageous bids that buyers make, hoping you will take the bait. One ruse is to have two different "buyers" visit your house and make low-ball offers. Then a third buyer, a confederate of theirs, comes along and makes another low offer, trusting that you will be discouraged enough to accept a very low bid.

If You Don't Sell the House

You are not required to sell the house. But you are required to repay the loan, up to the value of the house.

In your will, you could leave instructions that other assets of yours are to be sold to pay off the loan, so your heirs can inherit the house. Check with your heirs first.

Your heirs might inherit the house and then use a traditional or forward mortgage to pay off the loan, assuming that the house has kept its value. Then one of your heirs can live in it, perhaps paying rent to the other heirs. Or the heirs can simply rent out the house, holding it as an investment.

You or your heirs can repay the loan with other assets besides the house. If you own a second home, you could sell that and use the proceeds to repay the loan. Or you could sell still other assets you own, such as securities. This might be especially appropriate if you believe you don't need a second home now, or if you think your main home will appreciate more in the future. Heirs might sell their own home, if they own one, and move into the borrower's home.

If you sell securities to raise money, try to sell those on which you have little or no capital gains. Typically that will be bonds or bond funds. Try to avoid taking a nicely diversified portfolio and undiversifying it. And be mindful that securities that have sat there like slugs for years may be vastly undervalued, while securities with enormous capital gains may be ready to nosedive. There is an old saying: Don't let the tax tail wag the tax dog. But do keep tax considerations in mind when you are selling.

As it is, too many investors sell their winners and hold on to their losers. As Peter Lynch of Fidelity Investments has put it, people seem to be in the habit of watering their weeds and cutting down their flowers.

A reluctance to sell losers is clearly a part of the human condition. Here's a test to see if you are normal in this regard:

> You need $5,000. Right away. Maybe you have to replace your roof.
>
> You own a stock that you bought for $10,000, and it is now worth only $5,000. You also own a stock you bought for $1,000, and it is now worth $5,000. Which would you sell, the winner or the loser?

Most people would sell the winner, not the loser, even though selling a winner forces you to pay capital-gains taxes and selling a loser gives you a tax deduction (unless these investments are in retirement accounts).

Experiments have shown, in fact, that most people feel the pain of a loss twice as intensely as they enjoy pleasure from a profit. Richard Thaler, a professor of economics at the University of Chicago, believes that "loss aversion," as it is called, may be an inheritance from the days when we lived in caves, when any loss threatened our very lives—a loss of food, water, warmth, or shelter.

A friend of mine had kept much of his portfolio, worth several million dollars, in just one stock. He was a retired physician, a wonderful person in every way, and the stock was a renowned pharmaceutical company. "I know this company very well," he would tell me when I urged him to lighten up on the stock and to start selling some shares every year. "I know the people who work there, and I know the products. These are the most ethical people you could imagine. There isn't a finer company in the land." Then he would add, "My tax basis is around $1.40, and the stock is now $70 a share. Can you imagine how much in the way of taxes I would pay on my gains if I sold?"

When I give talks about investing, I sometimes describe my friend's situation. And I end by saying, "I won't tell you the name of the stock he so tenaciously held on to for so many years. But the name is only five letters, and it begins with M and ends with k."

"And it rhymes with 'jerk.'"

18

Advice for the Children of Senior Homeowners

If you and your brothers and sisters are well off, with no apparent current or future financial problems, you will surely not begrudge your parents enjoying a more comfortable life—dining out more, traveling more, putting another bathroom in their house, buying a newer car—and you would be happy to have them stop fretting about money, the way people from the Depression generation (like me) tend to do.

But you should also not feel guilty if you would love to inherit something of value from your parents. I certainly felt that way, and so do most children. After all, you want the best education for your own children; you want money to be there if your children have health problems. And a little cushion for your own old age would be nice.

Your parents or grandparents should think of your future welfare—and their own welfare. Sailing around the world on cruise ships and spending money on fancy new cars are perhaps not totally the right thing to do if these people have children with serious monetary problems and grandchildren with serious health problems.

A friend of mine, a retired physician, told me that he had given more than $100,000 to a neighbor of his who had a sick child. "If it weren't for me," he told me proudly, "that child would not be alive today."

I told him that he should have obtained written documents showing that the money was only a loan. And I asked him: how poor could that woman be if she lived in her own house next to his in that ritzy neighborhood? ("I never thought of that," he said, abashed.) And I reminded him that he had a granddaughter with a severe case of diabetes.

Stephen Pepe of the Community Service Network tells of an "uncomfortable" meeting between a potential borrower and the borrower's two daughters. One of the daughters approved; the other disapproved. "There was a lot of anger," he recalls.

Of course, some children go too far. One Wells Fargo agent told me that the son of a client complained to him that his mother was threatening his inheritance. "She's frugal. She doesn't need any more money." The agent said to him, "Is your mother's happiness less important to you than your inheritance? If so, I really feel sorry for your mother."

"Most adult children want their parents to be okay," says Bill Agner, director of reverse mortgages for the Mortgage Network in Indianapolis. "But I have gotten some pretty rough phone calls. They've called me everything, every name but the kitchen sink. I may say to them, 'Do you want to pay for their prescriptions?' One lady got a reverse mortgage, and her son called, asking, 'Did you make my mom a reverse mortgage?' I told him that I could not discuss that—it was a private matter. But he had seen all the documents.

"'Now she can't get another loan!' he said.

"'Why would she want another loan?' I asked. 'She doesn't need money now.'

"His answer: 'But *I* might need some money!'"

Counselors must be on the alert for children who intend to take advantage of their parents via a reverse mortgage, says Joseph DeMarkey of the Bank of New York Mortgage. It's fine if the parents want to buy a house for their child or send their grandchildren through college. But if an adult child has been living in the home for 10 or more years and is unemployed, there's the possibility of abuse.

Protecting Your Parents

Protecting your aging parents from crooks and scammers should be one of the duties of you and your siblings, especially if your parents have come into a tidy sum of money through something like a reverse mortgage.

If you don't offer to help your parents with their finances, what is the worst thing that could happen?

The answer from Michael Schulman, a CPA and personal financial specialist in Central Valley, New York, is: Your parents might get scammed. "It's the most overwhelming in terms of dollar loss."

"Older people are a favorite target of scam artists," Schulman went on. Urge your parents never to give out any financial information (such as their credit card and Social Security numbers) to anyone on the phone. Persuade them to take steps to safeguard their identities, such as by buying a paper shredder and using it on their old financial documents.

"There are a gadzillion scams," he said. Scams to get people to purchase a new roof or spring for new blacktop for their driveway. Or there's this ploy: Someone rings the front doorbell, and someone else enters through the back door and steals whatever can be stolen.

Then there are bogus bills sent through the mail. "Even I get bills for Yellow Pages ads I've never placed," Schulman complained.

He also gives this possible script: "I'm calling from your bank, and I wanted to assure you that we've gotten everything straightened out. Sorry if you've had any problems. The accounts had been fouled up, but everything's fine now. Phew! And to show how apologetic we are, we're even going to deposit $25 into your account. Now, would you read me the numbers on the bottom of your checks—to make sure everything is fixed now? Oh, and give me your Social Security number, please."

One of the concerns among people in the reverse-mortgage business is that older people, suddenly getting access to a good deal of money, will fall victim to scammers. Of course, as Sarah Hulbert of Seattle Mortgage points out, seniors are susceptible to scams whether they get reverse mortgages or not.

In fact, older people in general are especially subject to scams because

- They are more likely to be home during the day, available to telephone marketers and door-to-door salespeople. (I once paid someone to blacktop my driveway. He was a charming fellow with a winning smile, and the clincher came when he said, "Your neighbor over here has signed on, and I'll charge you the same as I charge him." My neighbor was an architect, very tight with money. A good recommendation. Later, my neighbor denied hiring the fellow. A successful con man, it is wise to remember, will lie with no compunction.)
- They tend to be lonely, eager to chat with people, eager to add some diversion to their lives.
- They are courteous and don't know how to dismiss someone tactfully, especially a friendly voice that says, "Joe, how are you this evening?" "Fine, how are you?" "Fine, thanks for asking! Joe, have you ever thought whether you have enough life insurance?" My own answer, as I said earlier, is to hang up the phone. And I don't care if the person said he or she was calling on behalf of the Committee to Send Civil War Veterans to Disneyland.
- Many older people are reluctant to talk about being defrauded. They are afraid that people will decide that they have become incapable of handling their own affairs, that people will blame it on their age. Says Dorothy Bargholz of the N.J. Division of Consumer Affairs, "When we tell them that most fraud victims are aged 18–35, it makes them feel a little better."
- If they have worked in certain professions, like teaching or health care, they tend to be especially trusting. All their lives, they have been encountering trustworthy people. Physicians are notoriously susceptible to being ripped off, partly because of their wealth but also partly because of their trusting attitude. (An insurance agent once told me, "I never try to sell life insurance to doctors. By the time they get out of medical school, they already have too much insurance.")

You might urge your parents to

- Never buy anything over the phone.
- Beware of tricky sales tactics, such as, "This is the last day of the offer."

- Get listed on the do-not-call registry—888-382-1222 or www.donotcall.gov.
- Have an exit strategy: "I promised my son, who's a lawyer, to check with him before I buy anything,"
- Beware of pitches even for such seemingly sensible expenditures as refinancing a mortgage, life insurance, and deferred variable annuities. (See Chapter 16.)

You might place "fraud alerts" on your parents' credit cards, and check their credit reports for unauthorized use. Remove their names from all preapproved credit and insurance offers. (Regarding fraud alerts, see www.fightidentitytheft.com/flag.html.)

Real estate frauds have become widespread in the first decade of this century. Crooks persuade older people to use their houses as collateral for loans, but set such severe conditions that the seniors may wind up defaulting and losing their homes. In one version, a balloon payment is required after a period of time—a requirement that the entire loan be paid off at once. This may lead to a new loan, with even harsher terms, eventually resulting in default and foreclosure.

Other frauds include:

- Nigerian frozen funds. About once a month, I receive an e-mail promising me many millions if I just send in some money to help unfreeze money in a foreign bank. Why I should be chosen for this honor is not explained, but amazingly some people fall for this trap.
- Viaticals, where you buy a life insurance policy on someone else—someone who is supposedly at death's door and who desperately needs quick money to pay medical and hospital bills. Naturally, these surefire situations are not offered by a legitimate viaticals broker.
- "Work at home and make $50,000 a year." The promoters require that you pay for materials and training first, and you never wind up making good money.

Many frauds involve unusual investments, such as foreign currency, commodities like rare gems, or private placements (investments that need not be registered with the Securities and Exchange Commission or a state agency).

Impress on your parents that they should be wary if anyone uses such words as "guaranteed," "risk-free," "act now," and, especially, "offshore." That word, writes lawyer Joseph L. Matthews in *Long-Term Care: How to Plan & Pay for It* (Santa Cruz, CA: Nolo Press, 2004), is used to explain why an investment is not registered with the SEC, as well why you would not have to pay taxes on the enormous profits you are promised.

Try to get your parent to promise not to invest in anything without running it past a financial adviser, lawyer, or accountant.

In talking with your parents, bring up the subject of frauds in general. Phone calls you have received about contests you have won, where you have to pay money to collect your award, or give your credit card number to pay for shipping charges. Or where you must submit to a high-pressure sales conference, or be obligated to make future purchases. I have heard of someone informed that he had won a boat, and it turned out to be a toy boat for a bathtub.

Then there's the person who rings people's doorbells collecting for a supposedly worthy charity. Suggest that your parents demand to see credentials. And if they decide to write a check, they should make it out to the charity, not to cash or to an individual.

The award for nerve goes for the scammers who want to help people recover money they lost in another scam. Sometimes they are the same crooks.

An alarm bell should go off in your mind if your parent suddenly develops a new close friend, a friend who spends a seemingly unending amount of time with your parent. In fact, your parent may seem to be under the thumb of this new friend, who could be either male or female. You parent doesn't do anything without checking with this new friend. Even before the new close friend gains access to your parent's checkbook, and begins writing checks to spare your parent the trouble, get help.

To deal with elder abuse, there are adult protective services throughout the country. Look up "adult protective services" or "elder abuse" in the government pages of your phone directory, phone the government's elder-care locator at 800-677-1116, or go to www.eldercare.gov You can get your state's elder-abuse hotline from the National Center on Elder Abuse at www.elderabusecenter.org.

For fraud in general, again check your local phone book, looking for government listings for help with consumer fraud or consumer protection. Also try your local prosecutor's office or your state attorney general's office.

Then there's the National Consumer Law Center, a nonprofit legal organization, at www.nclc.org/consumer/repair. You may be able to obtain the name of a local lawyer who specializes in consumer fraud. You can also file a complaint with the Federal Trade Commission's Consumer Response Center at 202- FTC-HELP. The National Fraud Information Center is run by the nonprofit National Consumers League; call 800-876-7060 or go to www.fraud.org/tips/telemarketing/investment.

For securities fraud, complain to the Securities and Exchange Commission at http://www.sec.gov or phone 800-732-0330.

Bringing Up the Subject

The hardest thing may be starting the conversation with "Mom and Pop, can I talk to you about your finances?" Even before talking with your parents, perhaps talk with your brothers and sisters. Agree on who will approach the parents and what questions to ask, such as:

- Do they have an up-to-date will?
- Do they have any life insurance policies, and are the beneficiaries up to date? (A secretary I know decided to check to make sure that her second-born child was listed as a beneficiary on her will. She learned to her shock that the only beneficiary listed was her first husband.)
- Do they have a living will, revealing what lifesaving efforts they may want made on their behalf?
- Do they have health-insurance policies, including long-term care insurance?
- Do they have a lawyer, an accountant, and a financial adviser, and what are their names and addresses?

In fact, inquiring about your parents long-term care policies is a good opening, especially if you, the children, offer to pay for it. Not many older people have such policies, and without them a serious illness could consume all of a parent's assets, leaving little or nothing for an inheritance.

Someone should get your parents' permission to monitor their finances, including their canceled checks and credit card statements. Schulman suggests looking for things like a payment of a thousand dollars to a Nigerian limited partnership, or a higher-than-usual payment to a nurse who comes in weekly. or bills from a telephone company in Minneapolis when your parents have been living in Boca Raton for three years. One counselor told me that a reverse-mortgage client of his had a painter who changed the $500 check she had given him to $5,000.

You might open a joint account with your parents, allowing you to pay everyday bills; when possible, arrange for recurring bills like (mortgage or utility bills) to be paid automatically.

Some other tips include:

- If your parents ever bring up the subject of a reverse mortgage and invite you to meet with their counselor, say yes. "Occasionally, parents don't want their children to know," reports Mike Gruley of First Financial Mortgage. "They don't want to bother them. But most children want to bothered. They would rather know ahead of time what's going on. If they are not involved, when they find out, they may be worried that someone is pulling a fast one on their parents."
- Ask your parents for a complete list of all of their assets and where they are located. Some of their savings might be in a shoebox under the bed or in the garage.
- Ask them for the location of their legal documents and insurance policies, and *verify* that what is at that location are the originals and not copies, which might not be as useful. And make sure the documents are up to date.
- Do you have a key to your mom and dad's home and car? If you live somewhere else and one of your parents becomes ill, you will need a place to stay and a vehicle to get around in.
- If your parents' finances are in miserable shape, maybe it's time to stop bailing them out. Federal, state, and local agencies are there to help people without assets if absolutely necessary. (See Chapter 5.)
- Consider having the parent consult with a financial planner so the burden of watching over the parents' finances falls to a neutral

third party instead of to an emotionally involved adult child. (See Chapter 7.)

- For a "care manager," go to www.caremanager.org. Click on "find a care manager" on the left side of the screen. Search by zip code or by city/state. Look for someone knowledgeable about your parents' special needs. Also click on "about your care manager" to learn how to select a care manager and what questions to ask.

Getting Power of Attorney

A member of the family should obtain a power of attorney for either or both of your parents, enabling that person to act on your parents' behalf when the parent is incapacitated. That person also should have guardianship papers, signed before the parent became incapacitated. The family member, if knowledgeable enough, can also help your parents with their investments.

Financial institutions that your parents deal with should honor a properly executed power of attorney form, but the process will be smoother if you make use of that institution's own form.

If the power of attorney was obtained more than a few years ago, have your parents update it or it may also slow down the process with their financial institutions. And if they spend time in more than one state, make sure that the forms meet the requirements of each state, or have a separate form for each state.

Your parents can obtain a reverse mortgage even if they are incapacitated, so long as someone has power of attorney.

Not advisable is a "springing" power of attorney, which goes into effect when someone is found to be disabled. A ready-to-go version is more efficient. With a springing power of attorney, there may be problems proving that someone is actually disabled on a certain day.

The power of attorney should be specific, giving the attorney the right to make gifts, for example, but perhaps within limits, say, up to $11,000 a year (currently the maximum tax-free yearly gift).

Glossary

Abstract of title A document listing the transactions affecting ownership (title) to a property, such as sales, liens, and mortgages.

Acceleration clause A provision in a mortgage that makes the loan payable right now—accelerates it—if (with a reverse mortgage) you haven't paid your homeowner's insurance or your property taxes, or if you haven't maintained your home properly.

Adjustable rate mortgage See ARM.

Affidavit of title A written statement that someone owns a property free and clear.

Agent Someone who acts on behalf of another person, such as when buying or selling a property.

Amortization The gradual repayment of a loan, each payment including interest and principal (the amount borrowed).

Annuity A form of insurance that gives you regular payments—typically monthly—for as long as you live. A variable annuity invests in securities whose value fluctuates, such as stocks. A fixed annuity invests in bonds. A deferred annuity is one where the payments are to begin in the future. An immediate or income annuity begins payments soon.

Appraisal An estimate of the fair-market value of something—what it might sell for right now.

Appreciation The growth in the value of something, like a house. See Depreciation.

ARM (adjustable rate mortgage) A mortgage in which the interest rate changes—rises or falls—in line with prevailing interest rates. The adjustments might take place every year. This protects the lender in case interest rates shoot up. The beginning interest rate on ARMs is usually low, to attract borrowers. See Fixed-rate mortgage.

As is No guarantees are made as to the condition of a property.

Assessed value For tax purposes, what a community believes a property is worth.

Basis For tax purposes, the cost of obtaining the property plus the value of any improvements.

Broker Someone who negotiates sales, as of real estate, for a fee or commission.

Cap A limit set upon how much the monthly payment or rate of interest on an adjustable-rate mortgage can rise.

Capital gain Profit on the sale of something, such as a house. It may be taxable.

Carrying charges Taxes, interest, and other expenses of owning a property.

Certificate of title A document attesting to the ownership of a property.

Chain of title A record of all transfers of ownership of a property, compiled from public records.

Clear title A title (ownership) that is free from encumbrances (problems), so that a property can be sold.

Closing The meeting at which a contract is finalized—and a reverse mortgage begins.

Closing costs The fees that someone pays at the closing. The amount can be covered as part of a borrower's reverse mortgage.

Closing statement A written statement of all the expenses relating to a real-estate transaction.

Cloud on title Any claim on the ownership of a property, such as a lien, that may reduce the owner's ability to sell it.

Coborrower Anyone whose name is on the loan document along with yours.

Collateral Property that serves as security for a debt, the way a house serves as security for a mortgage.

Comparables Other properties like the one being sold, providing clues as to the value of the property being sold.

Condominium (condo) A residence in which each unit in a group is owned by an individual rather than by an overall landlord (as in a typical apartment house) and in which the unit owner has an interest in the common areas (such as a swimming pool). Also, a unit in such a development.

Conventional mortgage A fixed-rate mortgage with a specified maturity date; also, a mortgage not insured or guaranteed by an agency of the U.S. government.

Cooperative (co-op) An apartment house owned by its residents, usually as shareholders in a nonprofit corporation, and managed by an elected board of directors. Also, a unit in such a building.

Counselor The Department of Housing and Urban Development requires that every applicant for a reverse mortgage consult a counselor for guidance.

Cream puff A house in good condition, in a good neighborhood—easy to sell.

Deed A written document conveying ownership to a property.

Default Failure to fulfill an obligation, such as to pay homeowner's insurance.

Deferred payment loan A loan to repair or improve your home, usually provided by the state.

Depreciation The loss in value of something, like a home.

Due-on-sale clause A provision in a mortgage contract that if a property is sold, the loan must be paid immediately.

Encumbrance A restriction on a property, such as a zoning regulation or a claim for payment (lien), that limits its value or use.

Equity Free-and-clear ownership of a property. Its value beyond any encumbrance like a mortgage or lien.

Escheat The state takes over a property when the owner dies and there are no legal heirs.

Escrow Placing money with a third party, to be held until title to a property is transferred.

Estate Someone's total assets—including securities, properties, insurance, automobiles, jewelry, and so forth.

Estate tax Federal and estate taxes on the assets of someone who has died.

Fair market value The price at which something can be sold between people who are not related and who are not required either to buy or sell.

Fannie Mae A privately owned organization subject to regulation by the Department of Housing and Urban Development. (The term is derived from "Federal National Mortgage Association.") Fannie Mae buys and sells mortgages.

Fiduciary A person acting on behalf of another and obliged to represent that person's best interests.

Financing Paying for the costs of getting a loan, such as closing costs, with money from the loan itself.

First mortgage The first loan that has property as collateral. Payment of the first mortgage comes before other, junior mortgages.

Fixed-rate mortgage The traditional mortgage, where the interest rate does not change, no matter what happens to prevailing interest rates. It has been described as "the devil you know." See ARM.

Floater Insurance that covers movable property, like jewelry, and covers it wherever it goes.

Foreclosure The procedure by which a property owner in default loses his or her interest in the property.

Forward mortgage The traditional mortgage, where a buyer pledges property in return for a loan, and repays that loan with interest over a period of time.

Ginnie Mae An organization that guarantees payments to investors who buy mortgage-backed securities. (The term is derived from "Government National Mortgage Association.")

Grantee The buyer in a real-estate transaction.

Grantor The seller in a real-estate transaction.

Guarantee The lender will be paid the difference between money owed and the selling price of property.

Handyman's special A house in poor condition.

Home-Equity Conversion Mortgage (HECM) The popular reverse mortgage sponsored by the Department of Housing and Urban Development.

Home inspector Someone who evaluates the soundness of a residence, recommends repairs, and estimates what the repairs will cost.

Home Keeper The reverse mortgage sponsored by Fannie Mae.

Home Keeper for Purchase A variety of Fannie Mae's Home Keeper.

Homeowner's policy Insurance that protects homeowners against losses due to theft, fires, storms, and other disasters.

Improvement A change that "materially adds to the value" of a house, "appreciably prolongs its useful life, or adapts it to new uses" (to quote the Internal Revenue Service).

Index A mirror of an investment market, such as the U.S. stock market.

Inspection An examination of the condition of the important parts of a property—the roof, the heating system, and so forth.

Insurance Partial or full protection against monetary loss—whether of life, health, property, and so forth.

Interest Regular payments that the borrower makes to the lender for the use of the lender's money.

Junior mortgage Any mortgage except a first mortgage.

Leftover equity In a reverse mortgage, money left after a home has been sold and the lender paid for his or her loan plus interest.

LIBOR The London Inter Bank Offered Rate is the interest rate at which banks in London lend money to one another. Financial Freedom uses this rate to determine its own interest rate.

Lien A legal claim on property because of nonpayment of a debt, such as by a repairperson.

Life-of-loan cap The highest that the interest rate on an adjustable-rate mortgage is allowed to rise.

Line of credit A credit line offered with a reverse mortgage. Minimum: $500 at a time.

Loan application fee A lender's one-time charge when someone applies for a mortgage.

Loan origination fee A lender's one-time charge for granting a mortgage.

Loan-to-value ratio The size of a mortgage compared to the value of the property. A house valued at $250,000 with a $200,000 mortgage has an 80% loan-to-value ratio.

Lump sum Taking your reverse mortgage loan in one single amount.

Manufactured home A house built at a factory, then brought to the building site. Also, factory-built.

Margin The amount targeted for a lender's profit. It is on top of the base interest rate. If the interest rate is 5%, the margin may be two points, so the rate is 7%.

Marketable title Ownership free of any problems (encumbrances or defects).

Maturity The date when the principal of a loan—the amount borrowed— must be repaid.

Mechanics' lien A legal claim against land and buildings on behalf of workers who say they have not been paid.

Mortgage A legal document conveying a loan of money, to be repaid with interest, and backed by a pledge of real property. A forward mortgage.

Mortgage banker Someone who initiates and services mortgage loans, doing the continuing paperwork.

Mortgage broker Someone who, for a fee, finds a lender for a buyer.

Mortgage commitment A written notice from a lender agreeing to grant a mortgage on a property for specific terms.

Mortgage insurance This protects you and the lender if your house is sold, and the proceeds do not cover the amount you borrowed plus interest.

Mortgagee The holder of a mortgage, such as a bank.

Mortgagor The borrower.

Nonrecourse loan. When you repay your loan, you can never owe more than the amount that your home sold for.

Options ARMs Adjustable rate mortgages that let a borrower choose which debts to cover with a payment—interest only, interest plus some principal, or less than the interest.

Originator The lender who makes a reverse-mortgage loan.

Prime rate The lowest interest rate that lenders charge—the rate their best customers pay.

Principal The amount of money a loan provides—before interest.

Principal residence A person's main residence, where he or she lives most of the time. Not a second or vacation home.

Proprietary reverse mortgage A unique reverse mortgage offered by a private company.

Realtor A real-estate broker who belongs to the National Association of Realtors and who has his or her own office. Real-estate agents work for Realtors.

Recording Filing documents, such as deeds, in the public records, such as those kept in a county courthouse.

RESPA (Real Estate Settlement Procedures Act) A law requiring lenders to inform buyers in advance about closing costs.

Reverse mortgage A loan made to a homeowner—paid monthly, all at once, or kept in reserve, or a combination—with the home as security. If the homeowner moves out or dies, the loan must be paid, perhaps with the sale of the house.

Right of rescission The borrower can cancel the contract within a certain number of days.

Second mortgage A mortgage in addition to a first mortgage and junior to it.

Servicing The maintenance of your reverse mortgage by the servicer—updating information, sending out checks, and so forth.

Supplemental Securirty Income (SSI) Government payments to the needy.

Survey A map of a tract of land showing its size, form, boundaries, improvements, elevation, and position relative to neighboring tracts.

TALC (Total Annual Loan Cost) An estimate by a lender of what a reverse mortgage will cost.

Teaser An unusually low interest rate on an adjustable-rate mortgage. It usually lasts for only a few months.

Tenancy by the entirety A form of property ownership by husband and wife in which, when one dies, the other automatically takes title—becomes the owner. Similar to joint tenancy.

Tenancy in common A form of property ownership in which each owner has a separate interest in the property. If one owner dies, his or her interest goes to that person's heirs, not to the other tenants in common.

Tenure payments The borrower receives monthly payments for as long as he or she lives in the house.

Term payments The borrower receives monthly payments for a specified period of time.

"Time is of the essence" A phrase in a contract requiring that the terms of the contract be performed by a certain date.

Title Legal ownership, as proved by official documents.

Title defects Claims, liens, and similar problems with a title.

Title insurance Insurance against a loss because of defects in the title. Someone might sell a property, then another owner might come forward.

Title search An examination of title records, usually at a county courthouse, to determine a property's legal status and rightful owner.

Torrens system In some states, a system in which land is registered so that the status of a title can be determined without anyone's having to search the public records further.

203-b Limit The Department of Housing and Urban Development's rule that every county has a limit on the amount of a reverse mortgage loan. The limits change every year.

Valuation The estimated value of real property.

Zoning ordinances A municipality's laws governing how land may be used. For example, prohibiting commercial establishments in a residential zone.

Appendix 1

Assessing Your Home

This questionnaire and the suggestions in Appendix 2 come from the WELLComeHome project, which was funded by the Retirement Research Foundation of Chicago, the country's largest private foundation devoted solely to serving the needs of older Americans and improving the quality of their lives. You can visit the Retirement Research Foundation home page at http://www.rrf.org.

Additional in-kind funding was provided by Ball State University, Department of Family and Consumer Sciences and School of Nursing. You can visit the Ball State University home page at http://www.bsu.edu.

This questionnaire asks the homeowner or caregiver to evaluate the rooms throughout the home to determine if one room or perhaps the entire home is a candidate for modification. The questions are designed to identify the simple things that can become obstacles as a person's physical independence begins to diminish.

To complete the questionnaire, get a tape measure and pen, and start a tour of your home. Follow the sequence of pages, measuring door widths, stair tread depths and heights, inspecting floor surfaces, etc.

The Entry

1. Is there a continuous hard and evenly smooth surface to the door?
   Yes
   No
   N/A

2. Are there any steps that approach the door?
   Yes
   No
   N/A

3. Is there a handrail or a grab bar along the steps or the ramp for stability?
   Yes
   No
   N/A

4. Is the pathway to the door free of obstacles (ivy, ground cover)?
   Yes
   No
   N/A

5. Is there enough room to assist someone with a walker?
   Yes
   No
   N/A

6. Is the pathway well lit during the evening hours?
   Yes
   No
   N/A

7. If there is a wood deck, are the deck planks even and not warped?
   Yes
   No
   N/A

8. Is a person in a wheelchair easily able to maneuver up the ramp?
   Yes
   No
   N/A

9. Is there enough room for someone assisting another to easily get in the door?
   Yes
   No
   N/A

10. Is the peephole on the entry door at a usable height?
    Yes
    No
    N/A

11. Is there a sidelight or window at the entry door?
    Yes
    No
    N/A

12. Is there a chair or small table near the entry to set articles on?
    Yes
    No
    N/A

13. Is there a doorbell at the entry door?
    Yes
    No
    N/A

14. How high is the threshold strip from the outside of the exterior door?
    Height of threshold _____

15. What type of door handles are used (round, lever, etc.)?

    _____

16. How many steps approach the door (i.e., the number of steps into the house?

    _____

17. How high are the risers on the steps?

_____

The Bathroom

18. Is there a need for open space under the sink or vanity?
    Yes
    No
    N/A

19. Are the faucet controls easy to use?
    Yes
    No
    N/A

20. Is the mirror at a good height?
    Yes
    No
    N/A

21. Is the toilet at a good height?
    Yes
    No
    N/A

22. Is the tub easy to get in and out of?
    Yes
    No
    N/A

23. Is there a tub or shower seat in the bathing area?
    Yes
    No
    N/A

24. Is there a nonslip surface in the tub or shower?
    Yes
    No
    N/A

25. Do you need grab bars by the toilet?
    Yes
    No
    N/A

26. Do you need grab bars at the tub or shower?
    Yes
    No
    N/A

27. If you have grab bars, are they sturdy?
    Yes
    No
    N/A

28. Is the toilet-paper dispenser within your reach?
    Yes
    No
    N/A

29. Are the towel racks at a good height for you?
    Yes
    No
    N/A

30. Is there adequate storage within your reach?
    Yes
    No
    N/A

31. Are the medicine cabinets within your reach?
    Yes
    No
    N/A

32. Is the medicine cabinet easy to open?
    Yes
    No
    N/A

33. Is there enough space to move around in the bathroom?
    Yes
    No
    N/A

The Bedroom

34. Is there plenty of circulation space around the bed and dressers?
    Yes
    No
    N/A

35. Is the bed at a good height?
    Yes
    No
    N/A

36. Are items in the closet easily reached?
    Yes
    No
    N/A

37. Are there shoe racks or shelves to get shoes up off the floor?
    Yes
    No
    N/A

38. Where is the master bedroom located (main floor or another level)?

    _____

The Laundry

39. Is the dryer at a height that is easy to use?
    Yes
    No
    N/A

40. Can you easily reach into the washer?
    Yes
    No
    N/A

41. Are the laundry detergents and softeners easily reached?
    Yes
    No
    N/A

42. Is there a worktable for setting laundry baskets and clean clothes?
    Yes
    No
    N/A

43. Do you use an ironing board?
    Yes
    No
    N/A

44. Is the ironing board manual or built-in?

    _____

45. What type of lighting is used in the room (task, single light)?

    _____

46. Where are the laundry facilities located (first floor, second, basement)?

    _____

The Living Room

47. Is there plenty of clear circulation space?
    Yes
    No
    N/A

48. How are the seat heights of the sofas and chairs (are they comfortable)?
    Yes
    No
    N/A

49. Is the furniture firm enough?
    Yes
    No
    N/A

50. Are the chairs or sofas arranged near windows to provide better daylight?
    Yes
    No
    N/A

51. Is there any type of level change in the living room (sunken or raised)?
    Yes
    No
    N/A

52. Are any of these lights operable by remote, clapper, or touch?
    Yes
    No
    N/A

53. Are the light switches easy to reach?
    Yes
    No
    N/A

54. Are the electrical outlets easy to reach?
    Yes
    No
    N/A

55. Are there area or throw rugs inside the home?
    Yes
    No
    N/A

56. Are the rugs secured in place?
    Yes
    No
    N/A

57. Can windows be easily opened?
    Yes
    No
    N/A

58. Is the window latch at a height that is easy to operate?
Yes
No
N/A

59. Are the windows double hung or casement style?

_____

60. How many lights are there?

_____

The Kitchen

61. Is there plenty of room to maneuver around the table in a walker or wheelchair?
Yes
No
N/A

62. Are the chairs' seat heights comfortable?
Yes
No
N/A

63. Are the chairs sturdy?
Yes
No
N/A

64. Is the table at a good height for getting up from the table?
Yes
No
N/A

65. Are there any obstacles in the paths between rooms?
Yes
No
N/A

66. Is there a hanging light over the table?
    Yes
    No
    N/A

67. If there is a hanging light, is it at a good height?
    Yes
    No
    N/A

68. Are the counters at good working heights?
    Yes
    No
    N/A

69. Is there adequate counter space next to the refrigerator, stove, and sink?
    Yes
    No
    N/A

70. Are the cabinets at a height that allows the shelves to be easily reached?
    Yes
    No
    N/A

71. Do any of the shelves of the lower cabinets pull out like a drawer?
    Yes
    No
    N/A

72. Can you easily reach the back of the lowest cabinet shelf?
    Yes
    No
    N/A

73. Could small items be arranged on tiers to keep them closer to the front?
    Yes
    No
N/A

74. Are electrical outlets easily reached from the counter space?
    Yes
    No
    N/A

75. While you work at the counter, sink, or stove, would it be easier if you were seated?
    Yes
    No
    N/A

76. Is there an open space below the cabinets to allow for seating?
    Yes
    No
    N/A

77. While you work at the sink, can you easily reach the back of the sink?
    Yes
    No
    N/A

78. Are the faucets easy to operate?
    Yes
    No
    N/A

79. Is there a garbage disposal? If yes, is the control switch reachable?
    Yes
    No
    N/A

80. While you work at the stove, can you easily see into the pots on the back burners?
    Yes
    No
    N/A

81. Are the controls for the stove easy to operate (grasp and turn)?
    Yes
    No
    N/A

82. Are the controls clearly marked for off and on positions?
    Yes
    No
    N/A

83. Is it difficult to reach in and out of the oven?
    Yes
    No
    N/A

84. Is the oven or stove installed at a comfortable height?
    Yes
    No
    N/A

85. Are the lower bins in the refrigerator too low?
    Yes
    No
    N/A

86. Are you able to reach to back of the refrigerator?
    Yes
    No
    N/A

87. If there is a food pantry, can items be easily reached?
    Yes
    No
    N/A

88. Is there a smoke detector?
    Yes
    No
    N/A

89. How is the room lit?

    _____

90. What type of lighting is used in the kitchen?

    _____

91. Can you reach the upper shelves or cabinets?
Yes
No
N/A

92. Is the refrigerator a side-by-side or is there an upper or lower freezer unit?

_____

The Hallway

93. Are there handrails on both sides of the stairway?
Yes
No
N/A

94. How wide are the doorways for each room?
Doorway width ____

95. How high are the thresholds to the interior rooms?
Height of threshold ____

96. How is the stairway lit (one single light or multiple lights)?

_____

97. How is the hallway lit (one single light or multiple lights)?

_____

The Garage

98. Is there room on both sides of the car to easily get in and out of the car?
Yes
No
N/A

99. Is there enough room to load a wheelchair or maneuver a walker?
Yes
No
N/A

100. Are there items stored in the pathway to the door of the house?
Yes
No
N/A

101. Is there motor oil or other substances on the floor that may cause one to slip?
Yes
No
N/A

102. Is there good lighting in the garage for entering and exiting?
Yes
No
N/A

103. Is there a handrail or a grab bar along the steps or the ramp for stability?
Yes
No
N/A

104. Are there steps into the house?
Yes
No
N/A

105. How many steps are there into the house?
Number of steps into house _____

106. How high are the risers on the steps?
Height of riser ____

Appendix 2

Home Modifications

To make a home safer and more comfortable for older people, here are changes suggested by the WELLComeHome project.

Bathroom

- Install grab bars. Place them in the bathtub, in the shower, and on both sides of the toilet. They would also be helpful outside the tub and shower for support and balance. (See "Grab Bars" below.)
- Increase safety with non-slip and slip-resistant mats and strips on the bathtub and shower and on the bathroom floor.
- Consider carpeting in your bathroom. It is warmer and may prevent falls. It gives people more confidence when entering and exiting a shower or tub.
- Provide either a transfer seat into the tub or a built-in platform. The bathtub should be a different color from the walls, and fixtures should contrast with the walls and floor.
- Construct a pre-built platform on the wall opposite the faucet. It should be at least 15 inches deep and made of tile or another waterproof material.

- A roll-in shower (one that a wheelchair can enter) is more accessible for everyone. For wheelchair users, the shower should have a five-foot turnaround. (This may include any area that is open next to the shower, if a curtain encloses the shower.) The minimum size of a roll-in shower is 2 feet 6 inches by 5 feet.
- A roll-in shower will have no curb or level change in the entrance, a gradually sloping floor and raised strip (maximum: half an inch) to contain water, and possibly a nonslip, waterproof "wet area" adjacent to the shower entrance.
- The 3-foot by 3-foot transfer shower with a seat is best. This shower has a specifically sized L-shaped seat on one wall, and the opposite wall has a precisely located set of controls and an L-shaped grab bar.
- Install a fold-down shower seat.
- Offset faucets and controls toward the outer edge of the tub or shower to make it easier for someone to reach the controls from the outside of the fixture.
- Install a hand-held showerhead with mounted clip holders. This enables those in a wheelchair or flip-down seat to better bathe themselves and reach the controls. A wall-mounted slide-bar can position the showerhead at many convenient heights.
- Install anti-scalding devices in sinks, bathtubs, and showers.
- Enclose the shower with a shower curtain. It is safer than glass and easily accessible, and can be maneuvered around transfer seats.
- Provide a raised toilet seat, which may be helpful to someone who has difficulty standing. Use a thicker toilet seat or spacer ring between the toilet rim and the seat. A conventional toilet can also be installed on an elevated base.
- Ensure that toilets are generally 18 inches high, no less than 15 inches or more than 19 inches. This enables those in wheelchairs to transfer easily from a wheelchair of the same height.
- Place the toilet in a corner for efficient grab-bar placement.
- Mount the sink on the wall or in a vanity with open space underneath. A removable vanity-base cabinet can create additional storage when knee space is not needed.
- Raise the recommended counter height for the bathroom sink from 32 inches to 33 inches from the floor; knee space should be a minimum of 29 inches from the floor.

- Enclose and insulate the sink pipes to guard against accidental burns or sharp edges.
- Install medicine cabinets so that they are easy to reach; mirror medicine cabinets are often at heights that are typically not accessible. A drawer or wall-mounted shelving for medications may be in order.
- Mount mirrors no higher than 40 inches off the floor.
- Arrange all water-flow fixtures so that users can operate them easily, with a closed fist, such as lever-style controls (as opposed to a round or square knob). With one hand in a single motion, the user should be able to adjust the controls.
- Consider other control options where feasible, such as push plates or electronically controlled systems where levels are preset.
- Create open floor space in bathrooms of at least 5 feet for a wheelchair turn-around.
- Remove locks from the bathroom door to avoid being locked in the bathroom.
- Change doors to swing outwards to avoid trapping anyone who has collapsed.

Grab Bars

- Use only grab bars with a diameter of 1¼ inches to 1½ inches. The space between the wall and the bar should be no more than 1½ inches.
- Properly reinforce walls to accept the load of the grab bar and the weight of a person.

Types of Grab Bars

- Wall mounted—most common and permanent.
- Seat mounted—fitted especially for the toilet; bars may wiggle or need adjustment over time.
- Floor mounted—often used near toilets and tubs and showers; permanent; may require wall and floor reinforcement.
- Folding or pivoting—wall mounted and can be moved when not in use; subject to maintenance and movement problems.
- Portable—movable, easily stored, and can travel with the user, attaches with combination of clamps, screws, or suction cups.

Further Suggestions:

- Install horizontal grab bars on all three walls of a roll-in shower.
- Install vertical grab bars to help someone maintain balance while standing, entering, and exiting the shower. Place adjacent to the controls or on the side walls.
- Provide four grab bars in a conventional tub; use only three if the tub has a built-in transfer seat.
- Two grab bars will easily fit around a toilet placed in a corner. Place one behind the toilet fixture and the other beside the toilet at a height of 33 to 36 inches.
- Mount a grab bar alongside the toilet at a length of 42 inches; the rear-mounted bar should be a minimum of 24 inches up to 36 inches long.

Bedroom

- Make a clear and simple path to the bathroom.
- Include night-lights in the bedroom and along the path to the bathroom.
- Add a light switch by the door and next to the bed.
- Include a five-foot turn-around space for easiest mobility.
- Allow three feet for wheelchair access on both sides of the bed if available.
- Install an adjustable hanging rod in the bedroom closet for people of all heights.

Entrances

- Widen walkways and driveways enough for a wheelchair to easily maneuver in these spaces.
- Clear pathways of obstacles, such as vegetation, stones, and furniture.
- Keep pathways well lit along the full length of the path.
- Maintain a minimum width of 36 inches for ramped entrances. When using handrails, the width should be 44 inches to 48 inches. Have guardrails and handrails on both sides along the length of the ramp or pathway. These handrails should be 34 inches to 38 inches above the floor surface.

- Be certain that ramps have a ratio 1:12; for every 12 inches of ramp length, the ramp should be raised in height 1 inch.
- Install handrails on both sides of the stairs leading to the entrance to increase safety.
- Maintain stairs so that they are even, sturdy, well constructed and comfortable, and adequately lit.
- Install flooring with a firm, non-slip surface of continuous texture, and keep it free of holes, bumps, or large cracks. The surface should also shed water and ice easily.
- Place furniture to allow for a minimum five-foot turning radius.
- Replace any warped or uneven deck planks. These can easily cause falls. Double-check that the remaining planks are properly secured and sturdy.
- Ensure that thresholds have little (half inch or less) or no level change at all.
- Adequately light the doorway for easier entry and to make visible the visitor waiting outside.
- Put shelves or a table near the doorway to free your hands when you enter the home.
- Provide a secured rug or another porous, non-slip surface to lessen slips and falls once inside.
- Set a second peephole at 42 inches in height, accessible to all wheelchair-bound individuals.
- Check to see if the doorbell or call box at the entry works.

Garage

- Clear any pathways of obstructions—especially pathways most often used to enter the home. Move the obstructions elsewhere or install shelves in an appropriate area that will hold these items.
- Thoroughly clean any spilled substances off the garage floor so that falls are less likely.
- Keep steps into the house clear; do not use them for storage. Add a handrail for easier use.
- Install a ramp if stairs make the garage inaccessible; make sure the handrails are accessible.

- Add lighting in the garage, especially along pathways most often used. Keep windows unobstructed to maximize natural light.

Hallways

- Establish a minimum width of four feet for all hallways and corridors.
- Install handrails in stairways, on both sides, to accommodate all users.
- Keep stairway efficiently lit at all times. Use nightlights as a backup at nighttime.
- Keep stairs clear so that falls are less likely.
- Remove any furniture from hallways or corridors and do not decorate these areas.
- Make sure thresholds do not prohibit easy and safe entry into each room. Remove or lower lips or curbs and clear doorway of loose materials (carpet, tile, or nails).

Kitchen

- Where possible, allow floor space of five feet in kitchens for a wheelchair to maneuver.
- Raise the toe kick to nine inches, as opposed to the standard 4-inch toe kick.
- Lower countertop workspaces to 30 to 34 inches in height, as opposed to the 36-inch height of standard countertops. To accommodate people standing, standard height counter segments can be provided.
- Eliminate sharp or protruding countertops; rounded edges help reduce injury in case of a fall.
- Increase the workspace; add a cutting board.
- Allow an area of counter space at least 30 inches in width, free of cabinetry underneath.
- Provide a rolling cart to help transfer large amounts of food to the dining space. The cart can be stored in cabinet knee space when not in use.
- Install an adjustable mirror over the cook top, to allow a person to see into the back burners.

- Install a counter-mounted stovetop, which is more accessible to someone in a wheelchair. It can be installed at a convenient height, instead of the conventional range height of 35 to 36 inches, which is too high for someone in a wheelchair.
- Allow for knee space beside a conventional oven for ease of use. Wall ovens and counter-mounted stovetops can have knee space below the appliance.
- Place controls on or near the front of the device to eliminate the need for you to reach over the burners. Where feasible, use a control knob with a lever handle or blade or electric touch controls because oven or stovetop controls are not easy for arthritic people to operate. Ensure that controls are properly marked "On" and "Off."
- Provide space under the cook top and sink at least 27 inches high and 19 inches deep, as well as 30 inches wide, so that a person in a wheelchair can maneuver under them.
- Allow at least 18 inches of working space on both sides of the stovetop, oven, sink, and at least one side of the refrigerator as accessible working space.
- Remove cabinetry from beneath the sink, and enclose or insulate pipes to protect you from burns or sharp edges.
- Install lever-style controls on all sinks as opposed to round or square.
- Place the garbage-disposal switch near if not on the edge of the counter to make it accessible.
- Use a sink with a basin of 6½ inches or less; it is more accessible to someone in a wheelchair because the required knee space is more easily provided.
- Where possible, put sinks or ranges in corners at a 45-degree angle to provide knee space and eliminate inefficient storage areas.
- When affordable, provide a side-by-side refrigerator, as it is more accessible than an upper freezer/lower refrigerator model.
- Replace the lowest shelves of the refrigerator with bins for easier accessibility.
- Select an oven or microwave equipped with side swing doors, which make transferring food easier.
- Store supplies where they will be easily accessible.

- Where possible, use Lazy Susans, a convenient way to store frequently used items.
- Make lower cabinets more accessible by replacing the standard shelf with a roll-out shelf or full extension drawers.
- Do not use upper cabinetry to store frequently used items.
- Use adjustable cabinetry that may be raised or lowered to an accessible height. The range of reach for a seated person is 15 to 48 inches above floor level. A standing person has a reach range of 2 feet to 6 feet.
- Use loop handles for cabinetry. These handles give people with arthritis a better grip on the handle. The preferred handle size is four inches, with a 1½-inch clear space between the face of cabinet or drawer and the handle. Handles should always be mounted as high as possible.
- Install electrical outlets in the front of the counter as well as along the wall. This lets people who are seated reach the outlets.
- Avoid using light-colored floors. They are more likely to show scratches and markings from wheelchairs and walkers.
- Take advantage of any natural light possible in the kitchen area. If not enough light is available, add additional light sources for proper viewing of difficult kitchen tasks.
- Regularly check the smoke detectors to ensure that they are working. Install an electronic system that will notify not only the resident but the fire department.

Dining Room

- Choose dining-room chairs with arms for support. The arms are most beneficial when they extend past the seat.
- Use a table 27 to 34 inches in height for accessibility; it should be stable enough to hold on to for assistance when you are standing.
- Keep the path between the dining room and kitchen clear so that no one trips or falls while transferring food.
- Remove bulky furniture or anything that may prohibit movement. Store china and other items in smaller shelving units or in the kitchen.

- Provide sufficient light in the dining area, especially in areas of activity.
- If a light hangs over the table, raise the light above the head level of someone standing, and make sure the light is anchored well in the ceiling.

Laundry

- Install laundry facilities on the first floor to allow for accessibility to everyone.
- Choose dryers that have swing doors on one side of the appliance.
- Install adjustable shelves that will hold detergents or other cleaning supplies.
- Allow space for an accessible table for ironing and folding.

Lighting

- Increase the amount of lighting.
- Provide consistent lighting throughout the home. Inconsistent lighting levels and brightness levels may produce frightening shadows, an optical illusion of steps or edges where the light and shadows meet, and—most commonly—increased confusion and agitation. Diminish glare. Reduced glare will maximize attention span and minimize falls and feelings of discomfort.
- Natural daylight must be accessible. Natural sunlight stimulates the circadian and neuroendocrine systems that regulate the body's entire homeostasis.
- Night-lights are needed to make a clear pathway during night-time hours. Night-lights help people avoid unnecessary falls and incontinence.

Living Room

- Do not change furniture layouts often.
- Circulation paths should be a minimum of four feet wide.
- Provide furniture that has arms.
- Avoid furniture with movement (swivels or rocks).

- Avoid furniture with sharp edges.
- Keep floor clear of obstructions to avoid accidental slipping or falls.
- If there is a level change, distinguish the edge or step with lights or railings to prevent falls.
- Make sure placement of switches allows lights to be kept on until the last person leaves a room.
- Switches, receptacles, faucets, controls, outlets, and thermostats should be mounted between 9 inches and 54 inches above the floor level.
- Warning signals must be both visual and audible.
- Ensure that all alarms work and have adequate power.
- Windows that are operable by the individual must not exceed five pounds of force to maneuver.
- Windows that have either push rods or cranks are most desirable. Make sure the window latch is at an accessible height.

Appendix 3

Helpful Web Sites

Reverse Mortgages

www.reversemortgage.org/
Excellent overview of what a reverse mortgage is, how to get one, and what it can be used for, with many testimonials from borrowers. Sponsored by the National Reverse Mortgage Lenders Association (NRMLA).

www.aarp.org/money/revmort/
Lays out in a systematic way the pros and cons of a reverse mortgage, as well as alternatives. Sponsored by AARP.

www.reverse.org/
Detailed information on all aspects of reverse mortgages: loan comparisons, life expectancy, interest rates. Sponsored by the National Center for Home Equity Conversion Mortages.

www.hud.gov/offices/hsg/sfh/hecm/hecmhome.cfm
Basic information on reverse mortgages. Ways to search for counselors and lenders, with links to other resources for housing for seniors. Sponsored by the U.S. Department of Housing and Urban Development.

www.elderweb.com/default.php?PageID=813
ElderWeb's page on reverse mortgages provides links to articles written about reverse mortages.

www.ftc.gov/bcp/conline/pubs/homes/rms.htm
Outlines the different types of reverse mortgages, along with advice on getting a good deal and avoiding scams.

www.hud.gov/offices/hsg/sfh/hecm/rmtopten.cfm
HUD's list of the top 10 things to know if you're interested in a reverse mortgage.

www.seniorjobbank.org/rm/index1.html
As a service to seniors looking to increase their cash flow, Senior Job Bank offers some basic information on reverse mortgages. There is a section on how to use a reverse mortgage with estate planning.

www.hecmresources.org/requests.cfm
Detailed information on receiving counseling for a reverse mortgage.

www.hud.gov/offices.hsg/sfh/hcc/hccprof14.cfm
For a HUD-approved counseling agency.

www.hud.gov/offices/hsg/sfh/hecm/hecmhome.cfm
To find lenders.

www.BankofNY.com
One of the leaders in reverse mortgages.

www.FinancialFreedom.com
One of the leaders in reverse mortgages.

www.SeattleMortgage.com
One of the leaders in reverse mortgages.

www.WellsFargo.com
One of the leaders in reverse mortgages.

Jobs

www.seniorjobbank.org/rm/index1.html
Jobs for older people.

www.retiredbrains.com
Job listings for retirees—part time, full time, or temporary.

www.thephoenixlink.com
Executives can post their résumés.

www.aarp.money.com
Companies, like Home Depot, that welcome older workers.

Public Benefits

www.eldercare.gov
For information on public benefits programs from your AAA (area agency on aging).

www.BenefitsCheckup.org
A Web portal that contains information and links to a wide variety of available public benefits.

Home Modification

www.bsu.edu/WELLcomehome
Comprehensive and top-notch.

www.design.ncsu.edu/cud
On home modifications, sponsored by the Center for University Design.

Budgeting

www.usaaedfoundation.or/financial/fin_retirebudget_budget.asp
A retirement budget worksheet from the USAA Educational Foundation.

Immediate Annuities

www.annuityshopper.com

www.totalreturnannuities.com

www.immediateannuity.com

Withdrawals

www3.troweprice.com/ric/RIC
How much you can safely take from your assets, from T. Rowe Price.

House Value

www.housevalues.com

www.homegain.com

Financial Advisers

www.fpanet.org
To find a planner near you.

www.napfa.org
Fee-only financial planners.

www.aicpa.org
CPAs with special training in personal finance (personal financial specialists).

Where to Move

www.bestplaces.net

Saving

www.nefe.org/latesavers/index/html
To help late savers prepare for retirement.

Appendix 4

Quotations about Old Age

Young-Old and Old-Old

In advanced old age, the chance of being physically disabled by illness increases dramatically. In part because of this higher probability, gerontologists often find it useful to make a distinction between two chronological subgroups of older adults: the young-old and the old-old. The young-old, arbitrarily defined as those aged 65 to 74, are often free from disabling illnesses. The old-old, those age 75 and over, seem to be in a different class. Since they are more likely to have impairing problems, they are more prone to fit at least the physical stereotype of the older adult.

–JANET BELSKY,
The Psychology of Aging:
Theory, Research, and Practice
(Brooks/Cole Publishing Co., 1984)

When a man fell into his anecdotage, it was a sign for him to retire from the world.

–BENJAMIN DISRAELI

Old age is not for sissies.

–UNKNOWN (sometimes attributed to Bette Davis, among others)

I've sure gotten old. I've had two bypass surgeries, a hip replacement, new knees. Fought prostate cancer and diabetes. I'm half blind, can't hear anything quieter than a jet engine, take 40 different medications that make me dizzy, winded, and subject to blackouts. Have bouts with dementia. Have poor circulation; hardly feel my hands and feet anymore. Can't remember if I'm 85 or 92. Have lost all my friends. But, thank God, I still have my driver's license.

—UNKNOWN

True terror is to wake up one morning and discover that your high school class is running the country.

—KURT VONNEGUT

Grow old with me!
The best is yet to be.
The last of life, for which the first was made.

—ROBERT BROWNING

Appendix 5

A $250,000 Reverse Mortgage

THE REVERSE MORTGAGE SPECIALIST* A SUBSIDIARY OF INDYMAC BANK, F.S.B.

Reverse Mortgage Calculator

Age Information:

03/19/1941   Nearest Age: 65
01/22/1935   Nearest Age: 71

Additional Information:

City/State: Woodstock , NY
County: Ulster
Home Value: $250,000
Liens: $0

	REVERSE MORTGAGE PROGRAMS ALL AVAILABLE THROUGH FINANCIAL FREEDOM™		
	FHA/HUD Monthly	**Fannie Mae** HomeKeeper	**Financial Freedom™** Cash Account™
CASH AVAILABLE			
Cash Available	$113,875	$31,927	$33,883
OR MONTHLY INCOME			
Monthly Income Available	$722	$269	N/A
OR LINE OF CREDIT			
Creditline Available	$113,875	$31,927	$33,883
Annualized Growth Rate	7.13%	N/A	5.00%
Creditline Value In 5 Years	$160,711	$31,927	$43,244
Creditline Value In 10 Years	$226,811	$31,927	$55,191
OR ANY COMBINATION OF THE ABOVE For example: 1/2 Cash Available, 1/4 Monthly Income and 1/4 Line of Credit.			

All numbers listed above are **ESTIMATES ONLY. This is not an offer to make you a loan, nor does this qualify you to obtain a loan. Interest rates vary by product and are subject to change.**

[< Back]   [Print]

Close Window

Appendix 6

An $800,000 Reverse Mortgage

THE REVERSE MORTGAGE SPECIALIST® A SUBSIDIARY OF INDYMAC BANK, F.S.B

Reverse Mortgage Calculator

Age Information:

03/19/1941   Nearest Age: 65
01/22/1935   Nearest Age: 71

Additional Information:

City/State: Woodstock , NY
County: Ulster
Home Value: $800,000
Liens: $0

	REVERSE MORTGAGE PROGRAMS ALL AVAILABLE THROUGH FINANCIAL FREEDOM™		
	FHA/HUD Monthly	**Fannie Mae** HomeKeeper	**Financial Freedom™** Cash Account™
CASH AVAILABLE			
Cash Available	$113,875	$57,012	$114,786
OR MONTHLY INCOME			
Monthly Income Available	$722	$480	N/A
OR LINE OF CREDIT			
Creditline Available	$113,875	$57,012	$114,786
Annualized Growth Rate	7.13%	N/A	5.00%
Creditline Value In 5 Years	$160,711	$57,012	$146,499
Creditline Value In 10 Years	$226,811	$57,012	$186,974
OR ANY COMBINATION OF THE ABOVE For example: 1/2 Cash Available, 1/4 Monthly Income and 1/4 Line of Credit.			

All numbers listed above are ESTIMATES ONLY. This is not an offer to make you a loan, nor does this qualify you to obtain a loan. Interest rates vary by product and are subject to change.

[< Back]   [Print]

Close Window

Index

Index

Index

Index

Index

Index

Index

Index

Index

Index

About the Author

Warren Boroson is a financial writer with the *Daily Record* of Morris County, N.J., and his columns are syndicated to Gannett newspapers. He is the author of more than 20 books, most of them about real estate, and is a former licensed real-estate agent. His articles have been published in *Reader's Digest*, the *New York Times Magazine*, *Woman's Day*, *Family Circle*, *TV Guide*, *Consumer Reports*, and other national magazines.

In 1996 he won the Personal Finance writing award given by the Investment Company Institute and American University. In 2001 and in 1990, he won the Rutgers/CIT award for best financial writing in New Jersey newspapers. He has also won awards from real-estate organizations.

Boroson has taught at the New School in New York City, Rutgers University in New Jersey, and Ramapo College in New Jersey. He was formerly on the staffs of *Money* magazine and *Sylvia Porter's Personal Finance Magazine*. He graduated from Memorial High School in West New York and from Columbia College. He lives in Hackensack, N.J., and Woodstock, N.Y.